PRAISE FOR THE AUTHOR

I did Alexei's 12 week course and it's really turned my life around. The whole business really, starting with sales process which wasn't really there and simplifying other processes. This has given me more time back, and helped us increase cashflow.
Curtis Lyons, The ICON Group

So much knowledge, very genuine, Alexei is a step ahead on so many levels.
Remy Durieux, Remy's Real Estate

Alexei and the team are quick and efficient and great to work with.
Lachlan Hardburg, The Autohouse

Alexei and the team are true to their word, they will bring customers to your business and know Google back to front. Highly recommended.
Luke Moody, Brisbane Supercars

If you're looking for an honest, ethical, helpful and results driven company for your Web and Online Marketing I strongly recommend that you give Alexei and his team a call.
David Myles, Gutter Knight

Working with Alexei and his team at Yews, has been the most profitable experience I have had in business.
Ben Purssell, LiveFit

I've personally used Alexei over a 17 year period and has easily increased the profits in our business by taking the guess work out of our online side of things.
Jason Urbanowicz, TrainerHQ

If you are looking to expand your business and expand your productivity come along to Alexei's Elevate Your Business workshop.
Kevin Gammie. Brisbane Small Business

I just attended Elevate Your Business by Alexei and it was absolutely awesome. I thought I knew a lot of this stuff, but I'm seriously impressed with the tips that Alexei shared. Alexei covered some impressive new methods for online marketing for any business and in particular using AI.
Matt Raad, eBusiness Institute

BETTER
BUSINESS
THAT WORKS

Creating Positive Change

GLOBAL
PUBLISHING
G R O U P

Global Publishing Group
Australia • New Zealand • Singapore • America • London

BETTER
BUSINESS
THAT WORKS

Creating Positive Change

How to fall back in love with your business while Getting Better Clients, Improving Sales and Creating Efficiency

FOREWORD BY
DALE BEAUMONT

ALEXEI KOULESHOV

First Edition 2025

National Library of Australia
Cataloguing-in-Publication entry:

Better Business That Works; Creating Positive Change
Alexei Kouleshov

1st ed.
ISBN: 978-1-925370-46-1 (pbk.)
ISBN: 978-1-925370-99-7 (ebook)

A catalogue record for this book is available from the National Library of Australia

Published by Global Publishing Group
PO Box 258, Banyo, QLD 4014 Australia
Email admin@globalpublishinggroup.com.au

For further information about orders:
Phone: +61 7 3267 0747

To my family for being there for me and supporting me through my business journey.

To my father who stood by me through every phase of life, even while facing his own battles.

To my team who made space for this book to be written.

To every business owner who refuses to settle for the average.

This book represents everything I believe about business: that it should enhance our lives, not consume them. That it should create freedom, not limitations. And that at the end of the day, it's the people we come home to that matter most.

Thank you for being my constant reminder of what truly matters.

ACKNOWLEDGEMENTS

As I reflect on the journey of writing "Better Business That Works," I am filled with immense gratitude towards a constellation of remarkable individuals whose support, wisdom, and love have been pivotal. This section is a small token of appreciation for the significant impact they've had on both my personal and professional life.

Firstly, I want to extend my deepest thanks to my family. To my children, Nick, Leon, and Vera, who bring endless joy and inspiration into every day - you are the reasons I aspire to create and leave a lasting legacy.

A heartfelt thank you goes to my mentors, Anthea Horvat, Jennie Gorman, Andrew and Daryl Grant, Darren Stephens, and Paul Blackburn. Your guidance has been a lighthouse in the vast sea of business complexities.

I'm especially grateful to Darren Stephens for organising the transformative event on writing a bestseller that set me on this path. To Andrew and Daryl Grant, thank you for introducing me to extraordinary individuals like Mal Emery and Greg Cassar through various impactful events—these connections have been invaluable to my journey.

I'm deeply grateful to Dale Beaumont for being an inspiration to both myself and my mentors. His outstanding events have been instrumental in building authority in the industry. Each of you, in your unique way, has contributed to the shaping of this book and the person I am today.

To my friends, Ilya Zakurdaev, Igor Komarovskiy, Natalia Demir, Daniel Herr, David Myles, Daniel Roberts and Will Rinas - your unwavering support and friendship have been a source of comfort and strength. Thank you for being there through thick and thin, for the laughter, the advice, and the memories we continue to create.

Thank you to my team at YEWS, Grigory Metlenko, Kai Yang, Max Koulakov, Luke Rankin, Liza Zemliana, KC Cruz, & Mervin Palaran and everyone else who helped me deliver digital marketing solutions to our clients.

A special thanks to my training partners from Legion FC and Atos Motavation BJJ. The discipline, resilience, and camaraderie I've experienced with you have not only kept me grounded but have also instilled in me a fighter's perseverance that transcends beyond the mats and into every aspect of life.

Most importantly, my deepest appreciation is reserved for my parents, Tatiana and Mikhail. Thank you for instilling in me the values of integrity, hard work, and authenticity. Your sacrifices, love, and unwavering belief in me have shaped me into the individual I am today. I am forever grateful for the foundation you've provided and the continuous support you offer.

To all mentioned and the many unnamed who've been part of this journey, your influence permeates every page of this book. Thank you for contributing to my story and for being an integral part of "Better Business That Works." Your support has not gone unnoticed, and I am eternally grateful.

With sincere appreciation,

Alexei

WHY I WROTE THIS BOOK

I decided to write this book because every business can do better.
Every business owner I met wants a business that works. A business
needs to produce satisfaction for the business owner and obviously
positive outcomes in the form of revenue. The revenue supports business
owners' way of life, allowing you to live the better life you seek. As well
as that, a business has to be an opportunity to invest in projects and
create assets for the future of the business owner and the company.

We found that the best investment opportunity for a business is to start
another business that allows leveraging more. An online store as a side
business would be a great example. Running such a business doesn't
require as much energy if set up correctly. The website carries out the
sales process, and you can delegate key activities, like marketing and
fulfilment, to others. This setup allows you, as the owner, to focus on
customer service and core transactions. These processes make up the
core of a business and consume less time.

So, Better Business That Works is all about you fine-tuning your
business, delegating through systems and processes and creating other
revenue streams. It's about bringing your business to a point where you
can focus on what's important. Once you have a business that works,
you can focus on streamlining and scaling it. If done right, this results
in more significant revenue and resources to start other side projects and
invest in other avenues. This is a real business that works.

FREE BONUS:
THE BIG PICTURE CHECKLIST
Fall Back in Love With Your Business

After working with hundreds of established business owners, I've identified the exact pain points that cause entrepreneurs to fall out of love with their businesses.

Your FREE bonus includes:

- The Complete Big Picture Checklist (34-point diagnostic tool)

- Complimentary Ticket to my next Elevate Workshop ($97 value)

- Free Access to the Better Business Community

This toolkit specifically helps established businesses (2+ years) identify:

- Why you're working harder but enjoying it less

- Whether you've built a true business or just bought yourself a job

- The exact area that's causing your biggest frustration

CLAIM YOUR FREE BONUS:

BetterBusinessThatWorks.com/bonus-offer

Use code: **BBTW2025**

CONTENTS

FOREWORD BY DALE BEAUMONT

Every so often, a book comes along that doesn't just offer advice—it offers a wake-up call. Better Business That Works is one of those books. It speaks directly to business owners who are working harder than ever but feeling increasingly disconnected from the business they once loved. Whether you're overwhelmed by day-to-day tasks, struggling with inconsistent cash flow, or simply looking for a better way, this book delivers insights that are both refreshing and practical.

What makes this book stand out is its clarity of purpose. It's not trying to impress with buzzwords or complex strategies. Instead, it gets straight to the heart of what business owners need: better clients, stronger sales, and systems that free up time—not consume it. The author's central message is simple but powerful: build a business that truly works for you.

Throughout the pages, you'll find a compelling blend of mindset work, time-tested frameworks, and step-by-step strategies. There's a strong focus on mindset—acknowledging that success in business often begins with internal shifts before external results follow. You'll also learn how to delegate more effectively, set meaningful goals, and apply the 80/20 Principle to identify what really moves the needle.

This isn't a book about quick hacks or vague motivation. It's about creating meaningful change by aligning your strengths, values, and vision with the business you're building. The author invites you to not just read—but to reflect, take action, and implement.

It's clear that a great deal of thought, care, and lived experience has gone into this work. The author has drawn on years of personal business growth and coaching to share a framework that's accessible to anyone—regardless of where they're starting from.

Whether you're just getting your business off the ground or looking to fall back in love with what you've built, this book will meet you where you are and guide you forward.

So if you're ready to stop running on the treadmill and start building a business that supports your life—instead of consuming it—keep reading. The answers are in here. But more importantly, the momentum starts with you.

Let this book be your roadmap—and your reminder—that it's not only possible to build a better business... it's within reach.

Dale Beaumont

Founder & CEO of Business Blueprint
Author of 19 Best-Selling Books

INTRODUCTION

This book, Better Business That Works, is a reflection of the coaching program that I've developed. I've been coaching and mentoring some of our clients over the last few years. Most businesses need better results because this will directly impact their personal lives.

I have been running my own business for over 15 years. My business is called Your Easy Web Solutions, which is a digital marketing agency. In terms of services, there has been quite an evolution in this business. We've gone through all sorts of things, like doing websites and driving traffic and conversions. After doing this for almost one year, we started focusing on improving the whole marketing process and working with clients to generate results. Most business owners who come to us want a quick win.

When seeking a better outcome for a business, the quickest win is always in sales. You will get a better outcome if you increase the sales conversion rate. This applies, of course, if you understand the value of your service and don't undercut yourself on price. This is, unfortunately, what many business owners tend to do.

You may not realise it, but you can usually outsource most other business areas. You can always purchase marketing and delegate things like accounting. Your main focus should be quality control on your business operations and sales. If you've started your own business, as I have, you'll find that you'll always do better at sales yourself, even if this is something you hate doing.

There were so many things I wanted to put in this book, but let's focus on what's been mentioned, which is to focus on the idea of building a better business that works for you. Why did I choose the name "Better Business That Works"? Well, that's what every business owner wants.

So where do you get started? It's really all about goal-setting. Many business owners jump into execution straight away. Only when things don't go according to their expectations do they try to look into why they are doing things in the first place. They try to figure out what they've done wrong, and sometimes it's just too late. I've met way too many business owners who are highly stressed out and are trying to make things work. Purely because they need the money, they rely on the cash flow that the business brings.

So to avoid all this chaos, you need to sit down and set some goals. Try to understand why you want to do things and whether what you are planning is the best way to do something. Business goals are about more than just the business. The business goals need to include a business owner as the person with the most gain from the business's activities. When a business gets big, this whole thing grows out of proportion. But that's a different conversation altogether.

Brian Tracy, one of my favourite authors, has a goal-setting concept called SMART goals. This approach enables clarity where the goals are specific, measurable, achievable, realistic and time-bound. This is an excellent way to get started, but there are more. Otherwise, you end up with many goals as dreams.

Once goals are set, many business owners struggle to understand if they're on track with their goals. Setting goals is one thing, but then breaking goals down into actionable tasks is where people start to fail. So, for example, a common goal is "I want a profitable business". What's profitable, and how much is profitable? Will this always remain the same, even when things change?

Usually, when you start, your mindset around business and goals is entirely different. Once you run a business for a while, you learn that some businesses are doing better than others. Some businesses are charging more, and some are charging less. It's great if you can offer a premium service straightaway and understand the value of your time and the solution that you offer. The reality is that most businesses start somewhere in the middle with their pricing structure (not that there is anything wrong with this). All you need to do is understand that once you start attracting clients in a certain way, it will impact the referrals you're going to receive in the future.

If you start selling on price or position yourself as cheap, this will reflect the types of customers you will attract. If all this is a part of the strategy, no problem, but just be mindful of that because too many business owners get stuck with mediocre clients because of this. Just think about why that may be happening. This all has to do with your mindset, which reflects how you believe in doing things.

Mindset is an exciting thing. Every person perceives things in a very different way. This is because of how you are brought up, taught and moved through life. It's not just about good and evil; it's about subconscious blockages preventing you from achieving more remarkable results. When it comes to pricing, people charge a fee based on their beliefs and the value of the problem they resolve.

Some people think that they're not worthy of certain things, and the personal side starts to impact business decisions. If you work in a team of people, you attract people who share or accept your beliefs. Forming one team working with one target market may not work if you decide to change things around and scale things unless you understand precisely how to influence and impact that initial mindset.

I've done a few programs throughout my journey, and in terms of mindset, it's imperative to be able to measure the actual changes. Your mindset is what connects you to everything else.

One of my business coaches introduced me to the concept of the 4Fs. Four critical areas of your mindset impact on your entire life. These 4Fs stand for fitness, finance, family and faith. Fitness is your health and well-being. Finance covers your savings, investing and cash flow. Family is people that matter to you and make an impact on you, and this isn't necessarily people who are blood-related to you. Finally, Faith is why you do things and the way you do things.

Faith is the most challenging part of the mindset. You may be a believing Christian and use many Christian fundamentals to do things; that's easy. Or if you've got your beliefs in a certain way because of how you've been brought up. Or it could be a combination of all those things. There's no right or wrong, and it's just more about understanding why things are happening in the way they're happening.

To stay on track with your mindset, you should regularly rate yourself in each area. Why is this important? Doing this will allow you to identify what's missing. So, for example, how is fitness right now out of 10? It's around five out of 10. Why is that? What would it take for that five to become a 10? These questions will enable you to identify the gaps.

My answer is that I need to exercise more and eat healthily. I've been working too hard and not sleeping enough. And there are a ton of other things that I shouldn't be doing. So, you'll immediately understand what you need to be doing to be that 10 in fitness. Hypothetically speaking, you never be that 10, as there's always something to do and improve. It's about understanding where you are and what you need to do to improve. With this method, you can measure up those other areas of the 4Fs.

So this is your mindset, and it's super important to understand what your current state is and what's limiting you. If you struggle with this, I suggest you find a coach who can help you know some of these limitations. Sometimes problems are self-evident and jump out at you when you try to do something. Other times they are not so evident, and you encounter the same set of problems repeatedly.

You're either unable to complete tasks, run out of ideas, or need ideas to start with. Sounds familiar? Throughout my business journey, I discovered something, and I've based my entire business around Wealth Dynamics. This concept was created by Roger Hamilton, an author and social entrepreneur. He has taken the personality test system Carl Jung and Briggs Myers developed and applied that to the entrepreneur mindset. This allowed him to establish personality profiles correlating to some of the most successful people.

You can identify your strengths and weaknesses by doing the Wealth Dynamics profile test. The system will also show you other entrepreneurs, you could be following to be more successful in your line of work. So I've done my test a while back now. I'm a Creator profile. My strength is really all about creativity, ideas and intuition. My main limitation is that I could improve at completing things. It's taking me too long to write this book. So learn to understand these things through tests like the Wealth Dynamics profile early.

Throughout my business journey, when I started in 2007, my most significant limitation was that I realised that I needed to be specifically good at finishing things. I was good at developing new ideas and doing the design side of things, but I couldn't execute what I'd come up with. I was my biggest enemy. Finding other people who enjoyed doing what I could have done better was the solution. I learned through Wealth Dynamics that most people who were good at completing the work I started were either Lords or Accumulator profiles. These profiles are entirely polar to my personality profile. This was the key that I needed to be able to build an agency.

Profiling systems like Wealth Dynamics can help you with your business. The Wealth Dynamics test is a simple diagnostic that enables you to identify these little things and put them in the grand scheme of things to make a difference.

So that is really the start of this book. I wanted to make sure that my readers understand in terms of references of where my ideas and inspiration come from. I follow quite a few people and consider myself a collector of ideas. Finding the right information and learning from the best people is the way to get where you want to be faster.

CHAPTER 1

THE WHY

CHAPTER 1

THE WHY

Why do we get into business? Every business owner has got their own story as to how they started. Behind every business, there's always a motivation.

For some people, it's simply about making more money. For others, it's a matter of trying to be free from the boss or to have flexibility around the time. The latter, unfortunately, often results in being a lot worse than being employed by somebody. For other business owners, it's a matter that they are not employable because of personal decisions made in the past, potentially making business their only option. So everyone has their own story.

Most people start a business with the realisation that they can do better themselves instead of working for somebody else. It's important to understand where in business you will end up when you make these kinds of decisions. In these situations, most people are self-employed. There's quite a difference between being self-employed and being a business owner. It's best to check out Robert Kiyosaki's **"Cashflow Quadrant"**. It goes in-depth about where people are in terms of cash flow, whether they're employed, self-employed, business owners or an investor. Why is this important? It comes down to being efficient and getting the most out of your time.

CASHFLOW QUADRANT

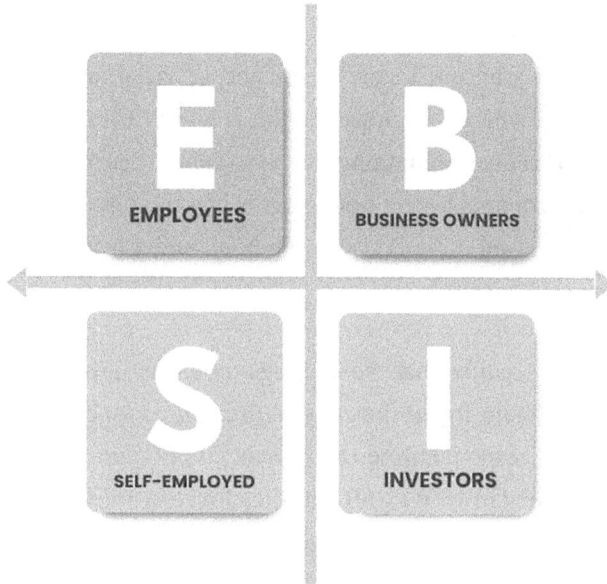

E EMPLOYEES	B BUSINESS OWNERS
S SELF-EMPLOYED	I INVESTORS

Focus and Specialisation

The ability to focus on business is vital. Many people start with one idea in mind, and as they progress, they pick up just about anything coming their way. This is because it's only a matter of time before cash flow, or lack of it, becomes a priority. As a result, many business owners really get stuck in this generalist environment where they do various services. Then over time, they would specialise in one or a few things that will actually do well. Many businesses, however, don't make it that far because they cannot generate enough revenue to cover their basic expenses.

Aligning Strengths and Delegation

There is quite a large gap between the idea of business and the actual business itself. For some business owners, it's probably a good idea to think about - why did I start the business? What are my goals, and how do I get to where I want to go with it all? With that initial idea in mind, is this idea even something that you want to pursue? Other people start a business at a relatively young age when their goals centre around thoughts like: I want a big house, a big boat, and a fast car. You get the idea.

Over time, they realise that these things aren't as important as others, and they completely forget their initial dreams. They become absorbed by daily family responsibilities and financial obligations and liabilities like mortgages and bills. With all this, they find themselves quite stressed and even burnt after a while because they get tired and haven't fulfilled their dreams.

There are a few things that lead to this tiredness and burnout. These things include poor time management and lack of goal-setting and focus. In addition, this could often result from the work environment, poor customer relationships, and other stress factors. The whole issue is much more complicated and goes far beyond just building a business.

However, there is a simpler way to approach this. Based on your strengths and weaknesses or your personality profile (something we'll cover in future chapters), you should focus on the appropriate activities that help you thrive and delegate the rest. This means focusing on activities you enjoy that align with your work strengths. Easier said than done, right?

Reviewing and understanding the initial "Why" behind your business is also essential. There's a great book I like to reference, which is called **"Start With Why"** by Simon Sinek. This book talks about the why behind much decision-making, and it's about being conscious of the central origin of ideas, problems, and desire for change. This book is a must for anyone who wants to do better at what they currently do.

Small businesses should be built around the business owner and their vision. However, you will likely become self-employed if you make it just about you. This differs from running a business. Being self-employed is about exchanging your hours for the income you receive. If you extract yourself from this self-employed scenario by taking a holiday or simply stopping working, you end up with either some clients needing more service or a loss of revenue. Getting back into this self-employed scenario restarts the whole process when you return. That's the main problem with being self-employed. Businesses have systems and people to solve this problem.

Building Systems and Teams

If you look at big, successful companies, they focus on ideas, systems, and people. If people are able to follow simple processes (parts of the system) and align with the business idea (vision of the business) - that's a win. If you understand this, it's only a matter of aligning the right people with crucial processes. Once people are aligned, supporting them with more systems around each of their roles is a matter of supporting them. Overall, it's a lot easier to employ somebody for a particular position as opposed to creating a role for a specific person. This is my experience from my observations and working with hundreds of businesses.

Right now in Australia, one of the most significant issues is the shortage of staff. Every single person who was thinking about doing something in terms of work has either found a job (or changed jobs) or started their own business. That's what it feels like, as every time I talk to people like this, there seems to be much change going on. It wasn't always like that, and the change in environment does get people to get their act together. This all reflects the mindset and the environment that people are in.

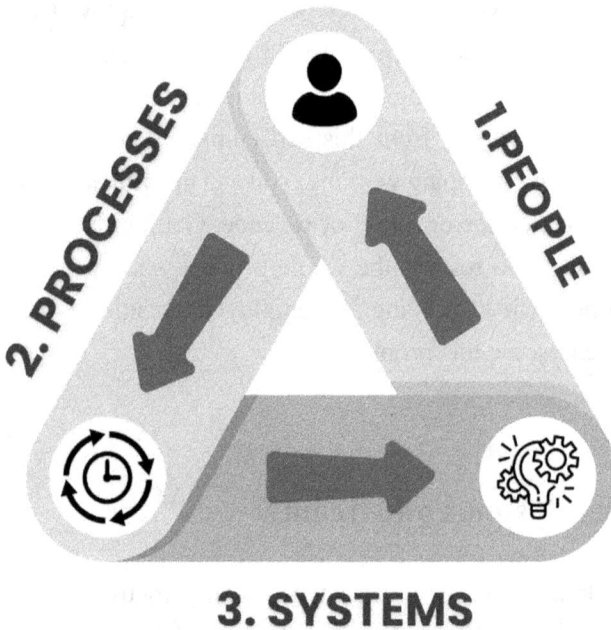

3. SYSTEMS

Be mindful of the people you surround yourself with. Having the right people surrounding you with the right motivation will give you more energy and create flow. As a business owner, it's critical to understand the right environment for your business. If you end up with people and systems in the right environment, it's just about your idea behind the business and your vision moving everything forward. If you still need to get that to start with, then that's something you need to address immediately.

If we are to do some analysis on the subject of why some businesses get bigger while others stay stagnant or die, we'll find a few exciting things. The businesses that grow typically are the ones that aren't afraid to let go. Things like delegation of tasks allow them to free up time and propel themselves forward. Another thing that stands out is the specialisation of the business and the critical focus on one of a few services.

As a business owner, understanding where you are and where you need to go often takes much work. Every day you are being stretched between various tasks and responsibilities. Education is the only way to find out and expand your thinking. That's right, by reading, going through courses and attending seminars. This is the fastest way. Behind this is a great concept that I like to refer to. This concept is called **"Who Not How"** based on another book by Benjamin Hardy. The beauty of the idea is that you can always get somebody who can do things a lot better than you, and if you can engage them, you will get a faster and better outcome.

Another bottleneck for many business owners is the misuse of perceived free time. This is when they aren't busy and are eager to get into areas of business that seem essential but where they need more knowledge or guidance. These tasks are like building a website, fixing your computers and doing your bookkeeping. While you may enjoy some of these things, doing them takes much valuable time that should be spent on generating revenue. This is where many startups get stuck, as they genuinely need help to get new clients.

Understanding Strengths and Weaknesses

It's best to understand your strengths and weaknesses early on and focus on things that you're naturally good at and that generate revenue. Otherwise, you spend much time on things you don't enjoy and often absolutely hate. Those are the things that you need to let go of and delegate. I use a personality profiling system for my businesses and the people I work with. It has served me well, and hopefully, it can help you. I will share more about it with you in the coming chapters.

So why did I decide to put this book together? The main idea is improving businesses and helping business owners align with what they do, love their business and get the outcome they should be getting. I call this Creating Positive Change.

Chapter Summary

1. **Reflecting on your 'Why' fuels long-term motivation and prevents burnout.**

2. **Self-employment traps you in a time-for-money exchange, unlike a true business model.**

3. **Effective delegation isn't relinquishing control; it's optimising your strengths.**

4. **Building systems and aligning people create self-sustaining growth.**

5. **Specialising in core services and continuous learning drives business growth.**

CHAPTER 2

THE PROBLEM

CHAPTER 2

THE PROBLEM

The Problem with Your Business

The problem with the business that you're running right now is that it probably isn't where you want it to be. More often than not, business owners fail to understand that they're heading in the wrong direction to where they initially wanted to go.

Business is a reflection of the business owner's mindset that they put into the business, whether it's your beliefs, your understanding of things or your view as to how you do things. This is why we end up with so many different businesses and approaches to fixing the same problem.

Every business is set up around a problem that the customers want to be resolved. Providing a solution is how you end up with a service. For example, with cleaning, someone's got a home that needs cleaning, and you've got the solution. With accounting, someone's got more understanding of how to get the best out of your tax return, and that is the problem, and an accountant is offering a solution to that.

Another example is a builder that has got the tools, the knowledge and the team to be able to build a house according to your needs. It's essential to understand the actual problem with your business and realise that there is a need to change.

Self-Employment vs. Business Ownership

Let's be honest; you'd want to spend more time with your family and friends now and again. Your business is supposed to enable you to do that no matter what day of the week. Nothing should be stopping you from what you want or need to do. If you're working in your business like crazy, nine to five, Monday to Friday, and you're still not making enough money, you're still working.

Well, that's not a business; that is called self-employed. You created yourself a job. It's imperative to us if that's what you want because if you're talking about a business, typically behind a business, there's a desire to build something that will eventually serve you. It's about putting things in place so that others want to follow you and work according to your vision and principles. If you still don't know what the hell's going on, let's start by reviewing the vision.

Your Vision and You

Most business coaches start working with clients by defining their business vision and mission. Most business owners, however, need help to understand what that means. The simplest way to put this is that your vision is how you see the business as how it does things. Now the mission is the execution of your vision. The whole thing is pointless unless you understand the depth of the vision, the mission and how these things shape your business.

A business typically has a two-year period to prove itself and determine if you are on the right track. If you're not, and the business is struggling within two years, you'll probably throw in the towel and then do something else. At this stage, the vision of the business should reflect your beliefs and project them onto the business. This all needs to be aligned with the problem that you're solving.

Scaling Your Business

If you are passionate about what you do and have found an excellent way to deliver your service, your business model needs to change - so that you can serve as many customers as possible. If you don't address this and work alone, you end up as self-employed instead of a business. The main difference between the two lies in how well you can scale your operations by using systems and people. So if you're starting by yourself, you can only do a limited amount of weekly work.

Now if you really believe that you've got an optimal approach and other people can follow it, and you can serve ten times as many people, the only way to achieve that is by engaging more people. From there, you need to understand why people want to work for you. Is it the money? Is it how you do things or the types of clients you attract? Or is it the process that you follow? Or are there many other factors that sometimes you don't even think about?

Let's look at a business like a cleaning company. Understanding the actual outcome of the business is really to save time for people to spend this time with their families. Or something more significant, like having a comfortable, pleasant home to be in. Realising this changes the whole dimension of what the business does. Now if you are not just doing the cleaning but helping people out and giving them time back, it helps people in the business feel good about what they do. You can also use some of these points in your marketing and overall business positioning to attract suitable types of customers.

The Impact of Vision

The vision of the business is really about the important things that make a real difference. For example, to grow the economy and to move the entire world to create jobs. If you understand this vision as the business's backstory, then the whole thing changes. So the vision behind the business is super important. The real challenge then becomes translating that vision into the business, which is what the business owner needs to do regularly. Now, with all that in mind, you really need to ask yourself, why are you starting your business? Are you just wanting to make money? Are you just wanting to do something simple? If that's the case, maybe you should buy a franchise or get into the business already set up and take over.

Business owners usually jump into all business areas (at least at the beginning). Optimally, it's best first to understand your strengths and weaknesses as well as to understand where you could fit in. You may possess a skill set in marketing and design. By buying a franchise or going to a business that is struggling in those areas, you can change things around.

Marketing can be compelling and can do many things, like attracting the right clients and focusing on the right products or services. Sales is another vast area of the business, without which a business won't have any clients.

Ultimately, it all comes down to different skill sets and mindsets. Some business owners find sales to be super easy, while others want to avoid getting involved in sales at all. The key is to align yourself with the right areas of the business. This will allow you to be the best at what you do and delegate the other business areas.

On the other hand, if you are building a business yourself and want things a certain way, you should do the due diligence of analysing other businesses and figuring out exactly what worked and has yet to work in similar businesses. This may help you avoid repeating the mistakes that others have made. I am not suggesting copying other people's businesses, but I understand all the ins and outs of businesses comparable to yours.

The next thing you need to watch out for is good and bad habits. Bringing any habits into your business is then hard to change or even let go of. It's hard because people follow others who lead by example often and need to realise it. The key is to understand the actual habits that impact the business altogether---for example, things like time management, priority setting and communication.

Many people fall enslaved to their businesses, and this happens for several reasons. One of the main ones is that business owners start feeling guilty if they stop working or feel like things may fall apart without them. For example, some tasks will get missed, or people in the business may only be able to carry out tasks with you. The truth is that this is often a result of a lack of processes, poor delegation, and failure of the business owner to clarify and communicate their vision to the key people in the business.

Work to Live or Live to Work?

Work to live or live to work? This is a question my father would often ask me. It's just a great way to challenge yourself to understand why you do what you do. Or if you have the freedom to do what you want through your work. The basis of this comes down to the concept of work-life balance. Just ask yourself these questions. Are you balancing your work and life by spending time with the people you want? Are you focused on the things that you really want to be doing? Or are you feeling held hostage by your business because you must be doing certain things? Does your work allow you to do what you want to do in life? On the other hand, you need to be realistic and understand that certain things in life require self-discipline as no one else will do them for us.

So where do you draw the line? It's essential for people to understand the overall direction of where they need to achieve their goals. This direction should define what it is that you actually want in life. Some things that people initially identify as their goals, like buying a house or moving into an area they wish to, translate into security or a sense of belonging. Buying a dream car isn't about the car but about feeling better. And if you have yet to figure out precisely what you want to do in life, that's fine, as most people are also trying to discover this.

The main thing is understanding if the work you do or the business you run gives you the flexibility you need to live your life.

If you're already doing something, and you know you're getting pleasure from it, that's great. But if you feel stuck in something that burns you out or makes you hate what you're doing, this really needs to be addressed. Most importantly, you need to understand where this is all going if you don't address these problems. And if you were to double, triple or even quadruple your business, what would happen then?

Unfortunately, many business owners need to be more consumed by their businesses. As a result, they need to be wearing more hats. They are commonly engaged in marketing, sales, and reconciliation; they are motivating the employees and doing hundreds of other things. However, if this all gets you satisfaction, it gets you the kick, and you feel like this is what you want to do. No problem. However, it may be just a matter of time until you realise you got tired. And taking a break from this all becomes nearly impossible as it would feel that the entire business would crumble like a house of cards.

Time is Everything

What would you do if you had more free time on your hands? Unfortunately, most business owners would spend their free time doing things they need to catch up on. That's not really how it's supposed to be. Ideally, we should focus on things that move us forward instead of things that make us stuck or even take us back. One of the main reasons people start businesses is to have more free time. Well, at least that's what the majority of people want. You want to be able to do things you want when you want to do them. And if you are clear about what you want, you'll sooner or later realise that there's a better way to run your business.

If you want to improve anything, you must realise that time management is the starting point. Take the time to analyse this problem, devise a plan and then implement your solution. There are simple inefficiencies in every business that can be easily fixed by better time management---for example, things like multitasking, poor scheduling for tasks and distractions of team members through occasional interruptions. Sometimes implementing time management principles requires foundational changes.

There are many great approaches, and when it comes to time management and improving business, I recommend starting with the 80/20 principle. I found that teaching my team about the 80/20 principles has allowed my guys to focus on the main things and be more efficient, particularly from the perspective of being able to delegate some tasks that are time-consuming, difficult and often simply not in line with the strengths of my team.

If you think of your role in business as the captain of the ship, you need to get a number of things straight. Firstly, the direction of where you are taking your vessel needs to be clear, as people need to follow your path and your lead. Secondly, you need to inspire, educate and motivate your crew in order for them to align with your business vision. Finally, the ship's captain needs the right tools and guidance to reach the desired destination. This all requires good time management and communication skills.

Let's look at a business like Google, for example. You've got two guys, two founders, currently projecting the vision into 10s of 1000s employees worldwide. And they do this really well. Working with Google made me realise that things can be done on a scale through clarity, motivation and innovation. Did you know that Google founders record a video every single morning for the staff worldwide about the changes that are taking place in the company and the things that they're working on? This allows them to connect with the entire Google team and be on the same page with them. It's really quite fascinating. From there, everyone's day is shaped according to their and colleagues' schedules.

So I think if you learn to manage your time better, you should be able to get more out of your day simply. The key is to focus on the right things that align with your personality and strength. Then make sure that you're not jeopardising your own time and you're not doing things at the expense of not taking holidays and not spending time with your family because that's what the whole business should be about. Ensure you understand that time is essential, and we only have a minimal amount.

Start With 80/20

Let's start with the 80/20 principle. The way this chapter is laid out, which is called The Problem, is all about understanding your vision. Whether you live to work or work to live, make sure that you know the whole element of time involved. And then, most importantly, understand where you need to go with all that. Now, the basic principle that works and applies very well is the good old 80/20. There is a book written in 1997 by Richard Koch called **"The 80/20 Principle"**, which outlines the good old Pareto Principle in line with modern business examples. Wilfredo Pareto was an Italian mathematician who analysed economics and found that there was always a principle where 80% of the results were brought in by 20% of the efforts. If you really look into this closely, you'll find that within your profit, 20% of your services will bring you 80% of your returns, and 80% of your problems will come from 20% of people.

With the 80/20 analysis of business services, one thing stands out. I like to look at this as the whole specialist versus generalist approach, which comes into where the services generating you a higher amount of money is typically from you being able to specialise in those services. So if you can let go of everything else, you become a true specialist. You can call this niche within a niche of your business or focus on the service area in your industry. The best example that I can give you of this is with specialist doctors. So, you can have a general practitioner, a doctor who charges relatively low compared to a specialist doctor. And if you're going to go to a specialist, this person wouldn't blink to charge you hundreds of dollars for a half an hour appointment. This is because they specialise in something you need a solution to, and you'd be listening to every word they say when you see them. So that's the difference between a generalist and a specialist you can apply in your business. You should always strive to be that special because this is where the 20% applies to you, focusing on building a profitable and scalable business..

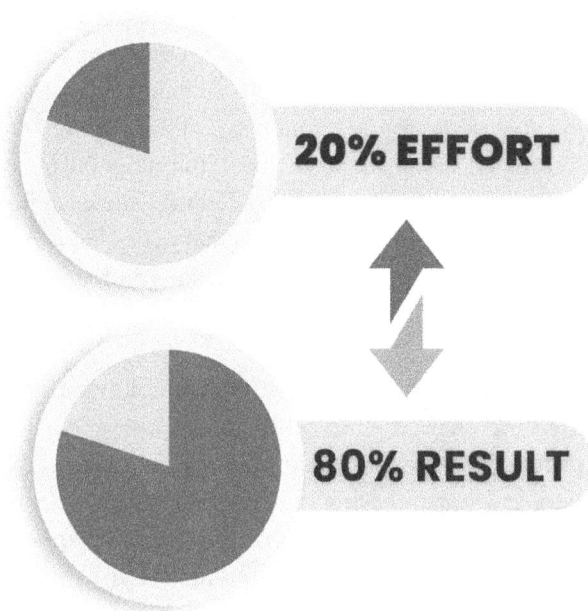

Now, if you're stuck in the same business in terms of being a generalist, here are a few reasons why. Most commonly, low-value customers will waste your time and not spend the money. If you continue with those non-ideal customers, you'll start getting referrals from identical types of people. An excellent example of this is getting referrals because you offer a cheap service. Also, if you start to do things in a certain way, you'll end up with many referrals and customers coming in that same way. So it's almost like you build a magnet that attracts the same sort of people, and I find that quite impressive.

If you feel stuck in a business that is not really getting you the money and you're wondering, where is all the money going? Well, I've got news for you, you're doing the same thing and expecting different results. Albert Einstein called this insanity. That was his definition of doing the same thing and expecting something different. It's evident once you look at it from a different perspective. You need to do that to see where the problem is. Sometimes it's not as obvious, and you need somebody else to give your opinion or show you the factors causing the problem.

If you've been in business for long enough, you've probably found your ways of putting out fires but not knowing the source of your problems. The first thing you need to do if you want to change is to stop. Take this time to review your activities and your goals and see if they are aligned. If they are, look at the recurring problems within your business like lead generation, conversion rate, customer satisfaction and cash flow. For all you know, you may be running a business that everyone is happy about except the main person, you. This should make you realise that you've entered a rat race rather than a business.

80/20 can be a challenging exercise, but I have not met a single person who's regretted the change. Start working on your specialisation and time management and start prioritising things. Start saying no to non-ideal customers and start focusing on services you profit from the best. We all want to make more money while having better clients. We all want to spend more time with our families and do the things we enjoy in life.

Chapter Summary

1. **Your business is a mirror of your mindset. Reflect and realign.**

2. **Clarifying your vision transforms your business**

3. **Scaling requires understanding why people want to work for you.**

4. **Effective time management is a game-changer.**

5. **Your business should support your life, not consume it.**

CHAPTER 3

THE MINDSET

CHAPTER 3

THE MINDSET

Business success isn't just about having a great idea, a solid plan, or enough capital. It's also about having the right mindset. Your mindset shapes how you approach your business, handle setbacks, and, ultimately, whether you achieve your goals.

In this chapter, we'll explore the importance of mindset in business, focusing on priorities, balance, self-discipline, positive thinking, and delegation.

You'll hear many successful people talk about mindset. Most business coaches start by addressing your mindset and focusing on how you think and perceive the world. The right mindset is key to moving forward, experimenting, innovating, and doing things differently. Everyone has a story, and yes, everyone has baggage. But this baggage doesn't have to hold you back - it can make you who you are.

When starting a business, we often confront the beliefs we were taught or get stuck with common misconceptions, like "money doesn't grow on trees." Some beliefs are beneficial, while others hinder your business growth. We project these beliefs into our daily lives and decisions.

Mindset is where it all begins, and this chapter delves into that foundation. Mindset enables us to do certain things in our business. For example, every business has a fee structure.

The fees a business charges reflect its perceived value. Often, people undercharge because they undervalue their services. The right mindset helps you understand your worth and the value your results bring to clients.

With the right mindset, you can achieve great things in your business.

MINDSET AND PRICING STRATEGY

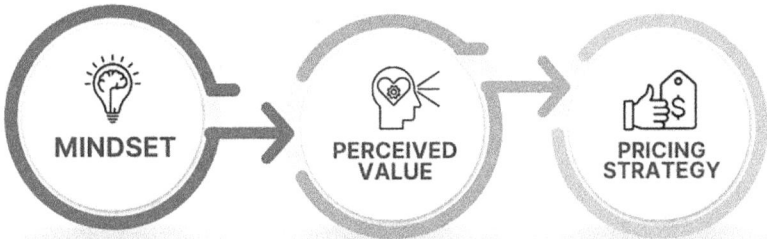

MINDSET → PERCEIVED VALUE → PRICING STRATEGY

Priorities

A successful business mindset starts with the ability to prioritise. As an entrepreneur or business owner, you will have many tasks and responsibilities. It's easy to get overwhelmed or distracted. To stay focused and productive, you must prioritise your tasks and activities based on their importance and urgency.

Prioritisation requires clarity of purpose, meaning you need a clear understanding of your goals and objectives. Knowing what you want to achieve and why it matters helps you make better decisions about what to focus on and what to let go of.

It's also essential to be flexible and adaptable. As your business evolves and new opportunities arise, you should adjust your priorities accordingly. Stay focused on your ultimate goals and make decisions that align with them.

While many decisions are based on intuition, especially in creative scenarios, a systematic approach can help. Tools like the **Impact-Ease Matrix** help prioritise tasks and projects according to their importance and the effort required. This visual representation aids in deciding where to invest resources for maximum return on investment.

Intuition is valuable but limited—it's like a muscle: effective but tiring if overused. Balance it with strategic tools to sustain high performance.

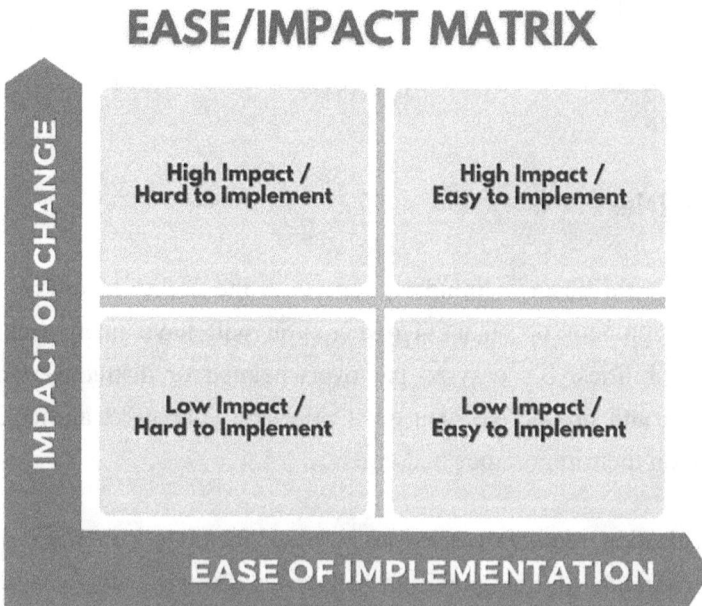

EASE/IMPACT MATRIX

High Impact / Hard to Implement	**High Impact / Easy to Implement**
Low Impact / Hard to Implement	**Low Impact / Easy to Implement**

IMPACT OF CHANGE

EASE OF IMPLEMENTATION

Balance

Another critical aspect of a successful business mindset is balancing work and personal life. Achieving work-life balance requires a conscious effort to prioritise time and energy across four critical areas: **family, fitness, finance,** and **faith.** Recognising that your business is not the only important thing in your life helps you make time for what matters most.

The **4Fs approach**—family, finance, fitness, and faith—can help maintain balance. This concept involves regularly assessing these four areas on a scale of 1 to 10 to understand where you stand and where you need improvement.

1. **Family:** This includes people who surround you and give you energy, not just blood relatives but friends and colleagues too. Consider the quality of time spent with these individuals and aim for meaningful interactions.

2. **Finance:** This covers your financial health, including cash flow, investments, and overall financial stability. Regularly assess and plan for improvements.

3. **Fitness:** Focus on your physical health, diet, and well-being. Identify gaps in your fitness routine and make necessary changes.

4. **Faith:** This is about your beliefs and motivations. Investing in personal development and continuous learning helps maintain and improve this aspect.

5. **Balance** is not about equal time allocation; it's about equal fulfilment in all areas of life.

Balance is not about equal time allocation; it's about equal fulfilment in all areas of life.

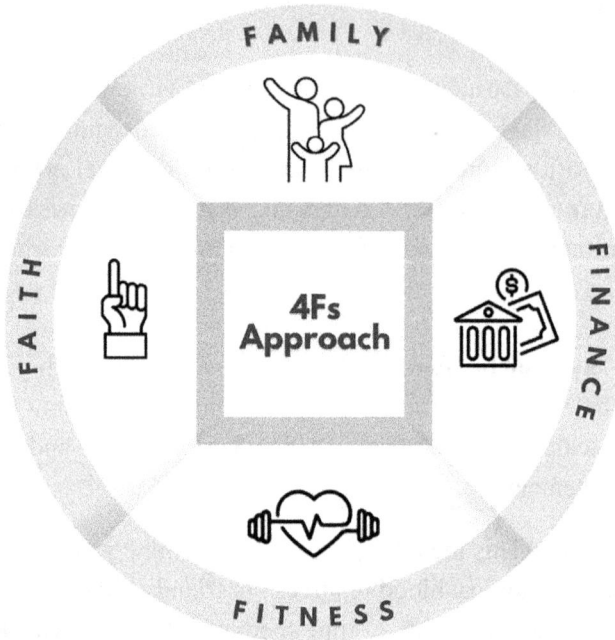

Self-Discipline

Self-discipline is crucial for a successful business mindset. It involves controlling impulses and staying focused on goals, even when faced with distractions, obstacles, or temptations. This is the most critical aspect of mindset—it's what allows some business owners to move forward while others get stuck.

Self-discipline means delaying gratification and making short-term sacrifices for long-term gains. It requires developing good habits, such as setting daily goals and sticking to a consistent schedule. For help with this, I highly recommend James Clear's **"Atomic Habits"**.

THE HABIT LOOP

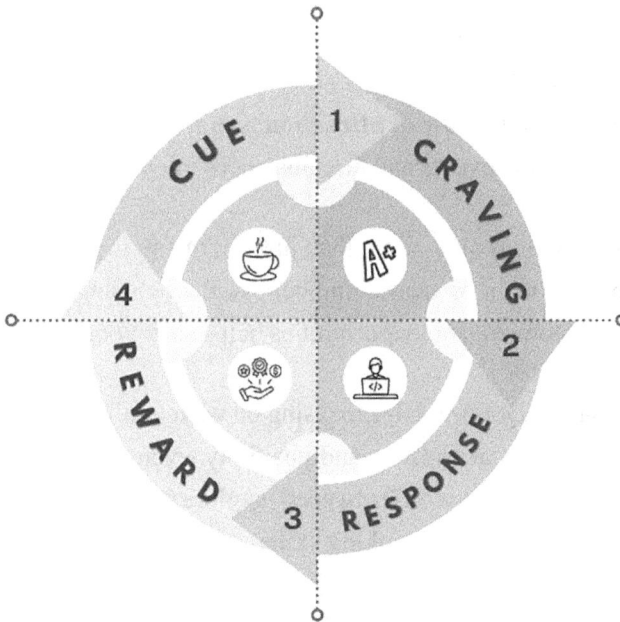

Self-discipline isn't about restriction; it's about liberation from short-term desires that sabotage long-term goals.

Developing self-discipline takes practice and effort. It can be challenging to resist temptation or stay motivated, but with time and consistency, you can cultivate the habits and mindset needed to achieve your business goals.

Self-discipline is also why many people seek coaches. Coaches provide accountability and help maintain discipline, propelling you to achieve your goals.

Positive Thinking

In business, mindset plays a crucial role in success, and one key aspect is positive thinking. Think of it as a magnet—focusing on positive thoughts and emotions attracts positive experiences and outcomes. This concept, rooted in the **law of attraction**, suggests that our thoughts and emotions shape the events and circumstances in our lives.

Positive thinking involves more than just optimism. It requires changing foundational thought processes and beliefs. Recognising the abundance of money, customers, and opportunities helps shift your mindset.

Practicing gratitude is vital. By focusing on what you're grateful for, you cultivate a sense of abundance and positivity, even during tough times. Resources like the movie **"The Secret"** explore the law of attraction and can help develop positive thinking skills.

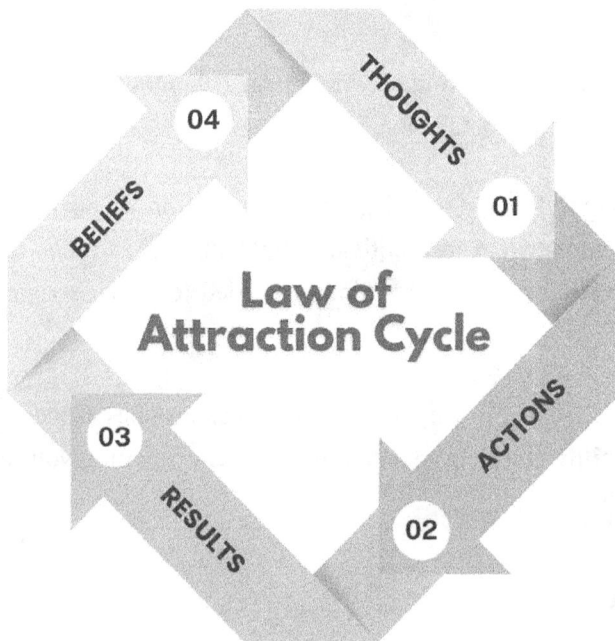

04 THOUGHTS 01

BELIEFS

Law of
Attraction Cycle

ACTIONS

03 RESULTS 02

Gratitude is a multiplier: the more you recognise your gains, the more gains you will see.

Sustaining positive thinking can be challenging, especially when influenced by your surroundings. Surround yourself with supportive, successful, and positive-thinking people to maintain a positive mindset.

Delegating

One of the biggest lessons I've learned is the power of delegation. Mastering delegation opens up endless possibilities for growth and success. Business owners often try to do everything themselves, leading to burnout and limited potential. Delegation involves recognising that others can perform certain tasks better and asking the right questions to ensure clarity and understanding.

If you find yourself doing repetitive tasks or struggling to delegate, it's time to step back. Delegate tasks that you don't enjoy or take up too much time to free up space and energy for what you love.

David Allen's **"Getting Things Done"** offers a great strategy for delegation. Having a clear flowchart for handling tasks ensures everything gets done efficiently and effectively. Delegate complex tasks or those involving others, and handle simple tasks yourself.

Delegation isn't relinquishing control; it's about optimising your control by empowering others.

Delegation is a mindset shift that can transform your business. Recognising your limitations and trusting others with specific tasks frees up your time and energy to focus on your passions. Always be grateful for what you have and focus on doing what you love. By mastering delegation, you can scale your business and achieve your vision.

GETTING THINGS DONE

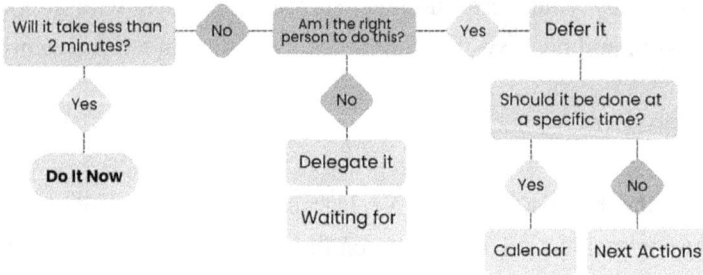

Will it take less than 2 minutes?	— No —	Am i the right person to do this? — Yes — Defer it
Yes	No	Should it be done at a specific time?
Do It Now	Delegate it	Yes / No
	Waiting for	Calendar / Next Actions

Putting It All Together

To summarise, mindset is a critical component of business success. By prioritising tasks, achieving work-life balance, and developing self-discipline, you can forge the mindset needed to achieve your goals and thrive in your business.

Mindset really is about what's stopping you and what's driving you forward. It's essential to understand your limiting beliefs and where you can improve. Making changes to achieve your goals involves recognising these beliefs. Jack Canfield's **"Success Principles"** is an excellent resource on the steps successful people take and the role of habits.

Remember, success isn't just about actions; it's also about thoughts. With the right mindset, anything is possible.

Chapter Summary

1. Balance isn't equal time allocation; it's equal
   fulfilment.

2. Self-discipline liberates from short-term desires

3. Gratitude acts as a multiplier of success.

4. Intuition is valuable but must be balanced with
   strategic tools.

5. Delegation optimises control by empowering others.

CHAPTER 4

THE SETUP

CHAPTER 4

THE SETUP

Goal-Setting

Setting goals is super important if you want to succeed in your business. The idea of goal-setting is about visualising your future and knowing where you're going. So goal-setting is about a better sense of direction and ensuring you're on the right track. Many people struggle with this and, as a result, completely disregard the whole idea of setting goals. The importance of goal-setting helps you understand what you're moving towards and why you are running the business.

Through my observations, business owners with clear goals usually perform better and achieve more. In any business, goals should include the size of your team, your revenue and the work environment you want. Other things to consider for goal-setting have the clients you want to work with or the partnerships you may seek.

From a personal perspective, setting goals is also essential. Is it a matter of buying a dream home, taking your family for a holiday, or buying yourself a car you're dreaming about? Set these sorts of goals to understand the results you will get from running your business. There are a couple of books that I recommend specifically around the goal-setting side of things. There is a book called Goals by Brian Tracy, one of my favourite authors. And he talks a lot about how to set goals specifically and how you can systematically achieve them. If you are stuck with goal-setting as a concept, I recommend that you read this book.

One common problem I often encounter is that people set goals that are too big. Break down those goals into smaller goals (or milestones) and focus on them. This way, you can see your results by achieving those milestones and feel you are on track. For example, improving sales in your business could be broken down into specific areas. This can be divided into training your sales staff, systemising your follow-up process, and increasing leads. On top of that, it would be great to measure each of the areas as much as possible.

If you want to enhance your goal-setting processes, try adding visual components. Some people use visual diaries; others do dream and visual boards. With dream boards, people cut out photos and pictures of the cars or houses they dream about and put them on the wall to help them better visualise their goals. As long as you stick to your goals and have the right mindset, nothing is impossible.

Ensure you find a framework for goal-setting that works for you. Once you've found it, commit to it. If you're serious about your goals, don't be afraid to declare them. That is one of the most powerful techniques that many people underestimate. Declaring goals is all about letting people around you know about those goals. You may feel discouraged by some people and even get pushback from your family and friends, and that's normal. It is your goal, and often, people look at you through the lens of their reality, and for them, your goals may seem unrealistic or even silly. The objective of declaring your goals is to make you accountable. It creates that accountability and pushes you more to achieve those goals. And if you do get discouraged by your friends and family, use that as the source of energy to achieve the goal and prove those people wrong.

One specific way I like to set goals is by looking at a goal and trying to break it down into micro-goals. These are the tasks required specifically around achieving that goal. From there, I look at each step and try to understand who is the best person that can help me achieve that faster. This usually results in getting the outcome better and faster. For example, if you are looking at buying a house, the steps would be: save for a deposit, find a mortgage broker to organise finance, find the right property and find a solicitor who can help me facilitate this transaction.

From this example, let's drill down on the goal of saving for a deposit. What would be the micro goals from this? What are my options? Do I need to save more, or should I ask my family for a loan? What's the process for me to get that initial deposit? The next step is a guy who is the person who can help me with it. Often, people need to realise that they can borrow from their parent's homes as long as their parents are okay with this. Once you understand the goal and break it down into tasks, get people to help you with those tasks. By getting the right people, you get a faster outcome and avoid much stress. The biggest mistake that people make is trying to do everything themselves. The issue with this is that people often need to realise the consequences of doing these things and realise how long things can take.

The goal-setting process outlined above is different from my creation. A good friend of mine introduced me to the concept of breaking down goals into micro-goals a while back. Recently, however, I was inspired by one of the books I've read called Who Not How. This book details finding the right people for your goals. So now you know where the ideas and inspirations come from.

Failing to achieve your goals is another huge part of goal-setting, and I like to look at it as a learning process. People are naturally hesitant to fail the overall look at this only from the negative perspective. Another way to look at it is that you can go to university and pay tens of thousands of dollars to learn something. You will end up with a degree and then get a job to get training, then again, before you start performing in your role. I would rather spend the energy to fail and learn from where I failed. This is a much faster way for you to learn.

For example, here is what would happen if you were doing digital marketing. You'd run some campaigns, ensure the tracking is set up so you can understand what works and what doesn't, and then from there you readjust your campaigns towards the desired outcome. The whole thing is applying your knowledge, experimenting, measuring and tracking to know that you're on the right path to reach your campaign goals. And trust me; you'll fail somewhere for sure. So failing is not a bad thing at all. What's important is to know where you failed and then why.

So, once you sort out your goals and start executing your micro goals, you'll be right if you go in the right direction. Then everything is under control, and failing becomes your learning trajectory. However, if you find that you're going in the wrong direction, you should reconsider the goal and stop what you're doing and set new goals.

Personality Profiling

One of the secret weapons in my business is the personality profiling system I use. This system is called **"Wealth Dynamics"**, which Roger Hamilton developed. Wealth Dynamics is based on the psychological types developed by Carl Jung. Personality profiling is about finding the synergy between your tasks and the people you work with. It is also a great system to align your team members and get them working with one another.

I discovered Wealth Dynamics in 2010 at a workshop I attended in Melbourne. This was by chance, as I was working on personal development and wasn't considering any personality profiling. I've since used this concept extensively to ensure that the people working for me are engaged with the activities to achieve flow.

Based on the personality profiles identified by Wealth Dynamics, this system works very well in understanding the future projection of how people develop in their roles. It focuses on role models of successful entrepreneurs that align with your profile. For example, Richard Branson, who is a Creator, is a great person for me to follow. Reading his autobiography is inspiring and helped me better understand some of my decision-making processes. This is because my Wealth Dynamics profile is also a Creator.

Every personality profile has strengths and weaknesses, and it is important to understand them. As a Creator, I am always full of new ideas and coming up with new ones is easy. I could improve at finishing things, so I needed a team to finish my ideas. It took me just over three years to find this since I started the business. I attempted to do everything myself and look while I enjoyed building websites and doing the technical side of things; I found that doing things took me a long time.

On top of that, my perfectionism would only let me finish tasks if I had to review them numerous times. This made me feel unmotivated, which was quite a common problem for Creators.

Many business owners are naturally creative and often have Creator in their profile. As a result, you are super motivated to do something every time. However, when you do it, you either get bored, your mind is elsewhere, and you want to do something else. For a creator, it is important to be clear on what you are doing and get into action quickly.

This action then needs to be translated into a tangible outcome. Otherwise, it becomes one of those many projects that must be completed.

Every person also has a secondary personality profile. It is similar to your main one, however, with a few distinct differences. For example, my secondary profile is Star. Now the Stars are genuine communicators and love good conversations. They say that the Stars don't shine light; in fact, they reflect light. This means that if you suddenly have the right person that a Star is speaking to, they activate. A great example of a Star is Oprah Winfrey. She interviews people, so she reflects other people's authority when she interviews them. Consequently, she becomes credible for the interviews, and her authority on many subjects grows.

Since discovering my Star profile, I've started doing much public speaking. Over time I found that speaking on the right subject and with the right people has enabled me to elevate myself and become an authority in several fields.

If you are a business owner looking for business growth, synergy or better team culture, check out Wealth Dynamics. You can take an online test that takes less than half an hour, and the results are instant. It's a multiple-choice questionnaire, and upon completing it, you'll get a document generated specifically based on your profile with references to famous entrepreneurs with the same profile. I highly recommend reading autobiographies of successful people with the same personality profile as you.

Wealth Dynamics personality profiling has been a fundamental concept for my business. Knowing my strengths and weaknesses and my team's strengths helped me avoid stress and chaos. The synergy of aligning the right team members with the right activities allowed me to create a good team culture. If you implement Wealth Dynamics into your business, you will build better trust between your team members, have meaningful conversations and have better focus. Most importantly, this should allow you to be happy by focusing on what you do best through delegating tasks to your team.

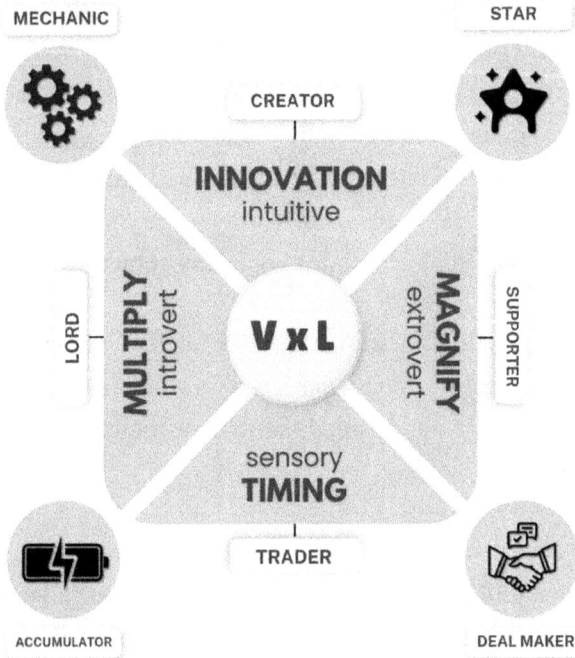

Time Management

Time management is one of the most important skills a business owner needs to master. Optimising your time to be able to work more and work more efficiently is the goal of time management when it comes to business. Even if you are charging well but your time needs to be managed properly; you often need consistent cash flow and a pile of outstanding tasks. I find that time management is the key to being productive and effective.

Here are a few tips to improve your time management. Repetition or patterns in your business is what you should be looking at if you want to start working on your time management. I've identified patterns in my business using Google Calendar, and I've noticed a pattern in the meetings I've had and those that converted into clients. I also found patterns in the team meetings and my personal schedule.

First of all, try to notice patterns in your business and create daily themes that would be best for certain activities. Looking at the diary of your past interactions is a good place to look for these patterns. Mondays are great for operations, while Thursdays are good for meeting and doing quotes. In my business, I focus on sales and meetings on days like Tuesdays and Thursdays, and having these conversations early in the morning works much better in terms of getting an outcome. Friday is a great day to do follow-up calls, and this is because people are a lot more relaxed. So if you are like me, sending out proposals on Tuesdays and Thursdays, then Fridays are ideal for closing sales. However, every business is obviously different. Then I looked into this particular pattern based on my previous calendar events, which is really helpful.

Put your personal and business events into your daily calendar. One mistake that many people need to correct is that they separate their personal and work calendars. As a result, they are unable to either include their personal events or forget about them.

Having personal events like meditation, gym, lunch, or family time helps you recharge and look forward to these things.

Secondly, break down your day into uninterrupted time intervals. If you find daily themes for your week and break down each part of the day into half-hourly blocks for tasks, this would allow you to improve things further. The idea is to have a visual diary of your day with a theme of the activities you should focus on in half-hourly blocks. This will allow you to stay in contact and remind you what you should be doing. This approach easily translates into the "Pomodoro technique", which Francesco Cirillo developed in the late 1980s. The idea is to work uninterrupted in 25-minute intervals when your brain is most efficient. A good plugin for your browser is **"The Pomodoro Timer"**.

Finally, and most importantly, have a task list ready at the beginning of each day. Rather than jumping into your inbox and seeing what needs attention, learn to plan ahead. Make sure you compile a task list and slot these tasks into the time intervals that you've identified. Please be realistic about how much time you would require for each task and also consider any other parties if they are to be involved in these tasks.

There are many things that could be improved by having the email inbox in front of you all day long. The biggest one is that you get emails that completely distract you from what you should be doing. Besides, the emails arrive in chronological order, pushing the older emails (often more important ones) to the bottom. I've seen people with hundreds of unread emails in their inboxes, and yeah, it just feels like an ongoing problem.

Are you a person who uses your email inbox as a project management or task management tool? Unmarking emails as tasks that need to be done? This is quite a thing with some business owners. The issue with this approach is that the task is not simply to reply to the person but also to carry out the task that is connected to the email. Some of these tasks are more complicated than others and require more time. This is why understanding your schedule and the time required for tasks to succeed.

If you are having the above issue with your inbox, here is a quick solution for you. Only check your emails at certain times of the day. Literally, focus on checking your emails only sometimes. Make the checking of the emails separate tasks and slot it into your daily schedule. A same-day or next-day response to most emails is reasonable. I typically check my emails in the morning (after I do my daily tasks) and then before lunch and at the end of the day. I allocate an hour for all these combined.

Some of you may have too many emails and may not agree with the above. You should review your business to see if you want to wear fewer hats. If there are genuinely too many emails, then perhaps you need to start by prioritising some times of emails (e.g. quotes and sales related) and creating a folder for all the interesting emails that can be attended to later (some call this the Swipe file - a collection of ideas).

The daily task list is the next part of time management you need to address. At first, this may take a little time, but once you get this gist, daily task planning should take 10-15 minutes. Start by identifying your tasks and creating a list of these. I'm old-school and use a pen and notepad for this. The next step is to identify which tasks are urgent and which are important. Prioritise the urgent and important ones and move the rest down the list. Alternatively, you can number your tasks in order of priority on the list you've put together.

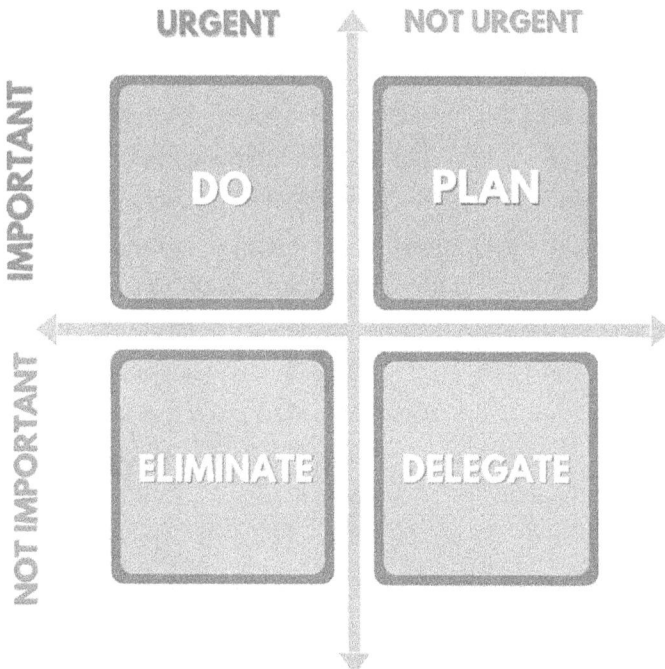

If you need help with prioritising your tasks, here are a few task themes that may help. Top priorities include cash flow, conflict resolutions and assigning tasks to other team members. These things typically take little time and require your full attention. Things that are important but can be done later are typically proposals, payments and setting up meetings. These are the things that may take more time but are optional to be done immediately. Other tasks need to be slotted into your schedule at a later stage or delegated to other team members (who may be able to do them better).

To summarise, time management is about having a clear schedule, a prioritised task list and working in uninterrupted chunks of time. If you understand the value of what you are doing and are able to increase your hourly output, you will quickly see the difference. If you want to explore this further, Greg McKeown has a really good book called **"Essentialism"**. This book talks about focusing on things that are essential in your business. I highly recommend this book.

The results of optimising your time management can be quite different. Some business owners find extra time to spend on their business, whilst others free up time for themselves. Each business has a lot of unattended areas, and if you spend at least half an hour per week on the areas, you can make quite a difference. You may find yourself involved in every task your team is performing or handling things outside of your skill set. To address these issues, I recommend looking into the concept of delegation. A great book by David Allen about this is **"Getting Things Done"**. You can Google up "getting things done chart", which is the main takeaway from this book. It's a flow chart that helps you identify the priorities of the tasks as they come in order to either do them, delegate them or bin them.

Time is what your business is really about. Most people get into business to have more free time. Whether you apply the above-mentioned technique or use something else, having more time is a huge win. Let's assume you free up half an hour daily, which equals over 100 hours a year. That's over two weeks of productive time that you'd save or invest in your business. So, please take time management seriously.

Key Areas of Business

In this chapter, I want to go over key business areas that need attention. Every business has four very distinct areas in it. Trust me; these areas need more attention and love to improve your business. These areas are marketing, sales, operations and accounting. Operations are your main skill or managing people who work under your command. This is something you have to be good to start with. This book is not about you doing better at your operations but about understanding the key areas in order to improve them. Once you know what the areas are in your business, you can work on improving them.

When working on their business, most business owners instinctively focus on marketing. This can be quite deceiving as every business needs to do better at their marketing; the problem is often much bigger than that. What most businesses need to remember is to focus on sales. More specifically, the consistency between sales and marketing. It's one problem not having enough leads, but how many is enough? The sales are the close rate between your enquiries and new transactions. Such businesses typically need to catch up, but rather than attending to this, they want more opportunities to have a crack.

There are a couple of areas where you can improve your sales process. First of all, review your close rate and the types of leads you are getting. The close rate for an existing business that provides quality service should be at least 25%. If you're doing lower than that, you're either in a very, very competitive market or, potentially, your sales process really needs fine-tuning. We'll cover the sales process in more detail later in this book.

The account area of the business is the most important area of the business since this is the revenue and profit of it. This includes things like your pricing, payment methods (and automation) and overall cost factors that keep your cash flow going. The whole accounting side of things is really different from my forte, and I've dabbled in this area in the past and have made the best decision on which way to outsource it. If you do, however, decide to keep this in-house, make sure you get the best advice and have some great numbers skills.

If you need to pay more attention to one of the four areas of the business, then this is where your business stops working. You need marketing to get sales, sales to do your jobs, and accounting sorted to make a profit from this all and adjust things. You can only do one with another. I've come across many businesses that have some areas that need to be remembered that consistently cause them issues. You may be providing the best service in the world, but if you are not invoicing timely or not getting paid, what good is it? So make sure you understand the whole sequence.

Now I love starting a conversation with my clients by asking them where the main problem is in one of these four areas. Among these areas, sales and marketing come up the most; however, problems in other areas can often be less visible. So let's go through each one of these areas and work out how these business areas and their problems interconnect. You may quickly find that your operations are what potentially helps you with your sales.

Marketing

Let's start with marketing. You are missing the point if you are trying to get it "right". Let's be honest; the meaning of the word "right" would need to be tailored to every industry and each business individually. Marketing is more about being effective and consistent. Many companies make the mistake of running marketing campaigns without split testing (testing various ads) for too long.

I like the old definition of marketing being **three Ms;** these stand for **market, media and message**. The market is your target audience, and it's best to be specific about whom you are targeting. The media are the channels that you are using to reach your target audience. Finally, the message is your ad that needs to consist of your business point of difference, customer benefits and a call to action. The three Ms need to be all considered as important; however, the message is the one that really needs more attention.

Even if you've been in business for a long time, make sure to define your target audience. Understanding your market allows you to achieve more than you may think. Start by going over your past transaction and understanding the profile of your customer audience (or audiences). Secondly, review your client's decision-making process to engage your business. Finally, knowing the type of persona you are targeting and their environment, you should be able to craft your message around them and use the right media channels to present your message.

If all of the above sounds too hard, or your business could be more complex, try the following. Go over your sales process to identify your unique selling points and also the tone that you use. See if you can include this in your marketing. This will allow you to plug your sales process into the marketing, which will help you increase the sales conversion rate through the theme of the conversations that the marketing message will initiate.

Here are some other tips that may help you strengthen your marketing message:

ACUA Principle

Over the years, we've come up with a concept called the ACUA principle. This abbreviation stands for Availability, Convenience, Utility and Affordability. This concept is based on the key areas of your marketing message that meet what the customer wants.

- **Availability** is how soon you can act on their enquiry and conduct the service.

- **Convenience** is about how easy you make the process for them; for example, you can provide an instant quote.

- **Utility** is all about the credibility and reputation of your business. This can cover things like how long you've been in business, being a member of relevant associations and having great reviews.

- Finally, **Affordability** is an obvious one which is about how affordable your service is. For some reason, many businesses need clarification on cheap and affordable. These are different, whereas affordable is about things like payment plans, taking various forms of payments and creating flexibility for the customer.

- We found that applying the ACUA principle in your ads is a surefire way to get a better response from your marketing campaigns.

ACUA, much like "aqua", is about flow. Everything has to flow towards the sale by aligning with customer wants. Starting with availability, going into convenience, utility and affordability. The basic idea behind this concept is about establishing a business proposition that addresses customer wants and creates a conversation about them rather than just the price.

"Empty your mind, be formless. Shapeless, like water. If you put water into a cup, it becomes the cup. You put water into a bottle and it becomes the bottle. You put it in a teapot, it becomes the teapot. Now, water can flow or it can crash. Be water, my friend." -Bruce Lee

---

Whether you are running an online store or a service-based business that needs leads, the ACUA principle can be applied to make a business do better.

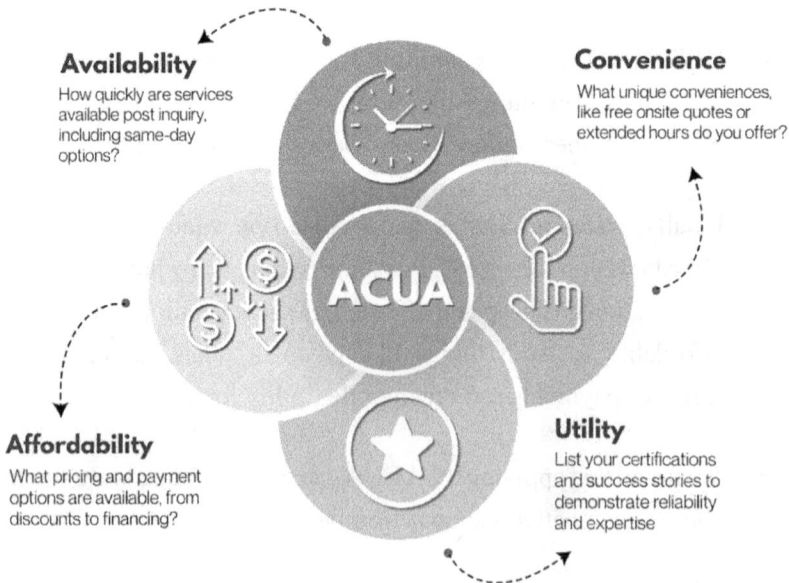

Availability
How quickly are services available post inquiry, including same-day options?

Convenience
What unique conveniences, like free onsite quotes or extended hours do you offer?

ACUA

Affordability
What pricing and payment options are available, from discounts to financing?

Utility
List your certifications and success stories to demonstrate reliability and expertise

Here are some things to stay away from in your marketing message. Even though things like "quality workmanship" or "great customer service" may sound like good selling points in theory, they are not and here is why. Customers can only experience these things when they engage a service provider, and there is no promise or offer that can give them confidence before the service is carried out. So you want to focus on the things that help the customer make their decision and give them peace of mind.

For example, here are some strong points that you can use in your marketing message to increase your conversion rate: **"7-Day Money Back Guarantee"**, **"3 Years Product Warranty"**, **"Local Friendly Team"**, and **"Payment Plans Available"**. Your entire marketing message that you're putting together should really be focused on what happens before the transaction occurs.

To get the most out of your marketing, understand your marketing objectives. Depending on your goals, your marketing objectives can differ; often, bigger businesses spend a lot of their budget on awareness and educating potential prospects about their brand.

I often see a lot of small businesses being caught out in things like outdoor advertising (e.g. billboards and bus adverts). The best objective for a small business is to focus on lead generation for their cash flow and ideal types of clients. If you've hit the ceiling and are struggling to get more leads despite increasing your budget, you should review your brand awareness.

Sales

Now that we've covered marketing, the next step is to address your sales area of the business. With sales, what you need to do first is define and understand your overall sales strategy as you focus on solving a problem (aka helping customers), offering a discount, using the GAP sales process (there is a great book on this called **"Gap Selling"** by Keenan) or perhaps doing a combination of these or other strategies. If you have yet to think of this and sales happen naturally, this chapter might reveal a few things you can improve on.

Depending on what stage of business you are at, you may need to look at your sales from a different standpoint. If you are a startup, this is something that you need to primarily focus on because if you can't close, it does not matter how good your marketing is. If you are an existing business, you must review your current sales conversion rates to see what can be improved. I come across many businesses (predominantly trades) that naturally have high conversion rates without even understanding the concept of the sales process. They think about it as helping their customers.

One common problem I come across a lot in sales is discounting. Although this can be executed as a strategy by some businesses to then compensate by upsells and repeat transactions. However, if you only focus on being the cheapest, this becomes a huge problem. The main reason is that some of your competitors respond by doing the same once you start undercutting on price. This price cutting, in the end, is simply the race to the bottom that has no real winners.

If you are intrigued by the strategy that may be executed behind discounting, here it is. Breaking down your sale normally consists of three parts: starting the conversation, educating the client and upselling by offering the right customer outcome.

For example, you may be offering a "20% off for new clients" offer which allows you to start the conversation with your prospects. Note that we are using a percentage discount instead of a dollar amount. What this does is that while it attracts the customer, it doesn't reveal the actual price.

Once the enquiry is received, the customer would be educated about the service to show them the benefits the business can help them achieve. For example, in a cleaning business, this could be a walk-through process that the business follows to address some aspects other competitors are unlikely to cover (e.g. shower screens and ovens).

Finally, upselling the customer could be an add-on service or a product bundled with the service initially enquired about.

There are three distinct parts of the sales process that I like to teach my clients. I call these the **three Cs of communication: Conversation, Connection and Conversion.**

1. **Conversation** is about building rapport over the initial enquiry and some social elements that may help the conversation. For example, with air conditioner installers, speaking about the reason for the enquiry (e.g. broken air-con).

1. **Connection** is all about creating trust and understanding the client's needs, for example, chatting about the actual problem or its effects on them and helping a client with their choice

1. **Conversion** is about offering a solution for their problem based on the ACUA principle and aligning it with the Conversation and Conversion.

CONVERSATION   CONNECTION   CONVERSION

There is another way to look at the three Cs regarding sales flow (of the funnel if you like). The conversation is the qualifying process that allows you to understand whether the lead you've received is right. The key here is to ask questions and listen. The most common problem at this stage is judging the prospect or just focusing on the information provided at this stage. The Connection is the education part of the process, allowing you to show the client your expertise and provide advice. The conversion closes the sale process based on the information gathered in the Conversation and Connection.

One part of the sales process that is often overlooked is the follow-up. If you are selling a high-ticket item (e.g. finance, property, machinery) that requires the customer to decide over a period of time, follow-up becomes critical. However, the follow-up, based on a conversation from a few days ago, could be stronger. The best way to follow up is to send a service proposal out after the initial conversation.

The proposal is an essential part of any sales process where the business wants an increase in its conversion. This works simply because most people are visual and need information in front of them to understand the information better and make a decision. A good proposal has key service parts covered, such as the overview of the business, its service process, credibility points and reasons why they chose your business.

Imagine a customer getting another sales presentation by reading your proposal. So if you are still sending one-page quotes or spending hours typing each proposal in Word, you need to do this right. Many platforms allow you to template your documents using the 80/20 approach. 80% of your proposal is a repetition of the same content most of the time. The platform that we use and recommend is **PandaDoc**. This allows us to cut down the proposal generation to under 10 minutes and provides analytics about user interactions with it.

Here are my top three if you are looking for book recommendations to improve your sales process. Brian Tracy's **"The Psychology of Selling"** is a great book about a systematic sales approach. Grant Cardone's **"Sell or Be Sold"** is a good source of ideas and motivation (listen to the audiobook). Finally, Zig Ziglar's **"The Secrets of Closing the Sale"** is an in-depth overview of mastering sales with many ideas and practical examples.

It would be best to look at the systems because, with every business, it's systems rather than people that are the only way to scale a business. So a lot of the time, people start to get more people on board without fine-tuning their systems. And that's problem number one. With a proper system, you're able to collaborate with the people. You have to clarify everything every single time.

So having a CRM or having some workflow system or a project, a basic project management tool, like **Trello**, for example, allows you to do many things. So what you want to do is go back to that goal-setting, your task setting example where you break a task into subtasks and essentially create a checklist or a task list if you want. And the idea is to assign that to a particular person so people can check it off as they go this way. You'll be sure that everyone's following a process, that they're missing parts, and that everything gets done.

You can also put things like deadlines on certain tasks. All ideas involve breaking them down and managing them in a team environment. There are many different tools if you're looking for some good suggestions. Some of them are free, some of them are paid, and some of them are free to a certain degree. We love using **Trello**. That's a good tool.

There's another tool called **Asana** that works similarly. It's all about boards where you can go into tasks and then drag and drop them into different stages. When a task is started, in progress, or completed, you should have a snapshot of what's going on as a business owner. Particularly if any completed tasks will free up time and allow you and your team to focus on the more important thing.

Operations

Operations management is the heart of any business and the key driver of efficiency, productivity, and profitability. The ability to master operations can make or break your business. In this section, we will touch on six critical elements that will help you to excel in operations management and drive success in your business. Each topic could be a chapter of its own, but I want to draw your attention to these.

Striving for Excellence

One of the most important aspects of operations management is to be good at what you do. You need to be more than average or good and strive for excellence. This means understanding your products or services inside and out, articulating the unique value proposition you offer, and continuously honing your skills to stay ahead of the competition. Being good at what you do is the foundation of success.

Specialist vs Generalist

As an operations manager, you must decide whether to be a specialist or a generalist. A specialist focuses on a particular area of operations, while a generalist is proficient in multiple areas. There are benefits to both approaches, but it ultimately depends on the needs of your business. Specialising in a specific area can make you an expert and give you a competitive edge while being a generalist can offer flexibility and the ability to handle various tasks.

Time Management

Time management is a critical skill in operations management. You need to be able to manage your time effectively to ensure that projects are completed on time and within budget. This requires setting priorities, creating schedules, and delegating tasks. Time management can also help you to stay organised and reduce stress, leading to better decision-making and a more productive work environment.

Team Synergy

In operations management, your team is your most valuable asset. Creating a culture of teamwork and collaboration can improve productivity and performance. It would help if you fostered an environment where team members feel valued, motivated, and empowered. This means promoting open communication, recognising achievements, and providing opportunities for growth and development. Team synergy can lead to a more cohesive and effective team.

CRMs

Customer Relationship Management (CRM) is a vital tool in operations management. It allows you to manage interactions with customers and potential customers, including sales, marketing, and customer support. CRMs can help you to streamline processes, improve communication, and increase customer satisfaction. Choosing a CRM aligned with your business needs is important. Also, choose a CRM that is easy to use and maintain.

Project Management

Project management is the process of planning, executing, and controlling projects from start to finish. It is a critical skill in operations management, ensuring that projects are completed on time, within budget, and to the desired quality standards. Effective project management requires strong communication skills, risk management, and adapting to changing circumstances. A project management system can help you streamline processes and improve efficiency.

Accounting

Accounting is the most important part of evaluating the outcome of your efforts and fine-tuning your business. Controlling the profitability of your business and being able to scale it are the main objectives. The good thing about accounting is that it's mainly about numbers, and numbers don't lie. There are, however, other aspects of accounting that require an understanding of timing, consistency and systems.

Accounting is not my forte, so I delegate it to an accountant that understands my business model and has the knowledge to support me. I recommend finding the right accountant for your business and outsourcing as much of it as possible.

If you think this chapter will be about numbers and profit and loss, I am sorry I have to disappoint you. Numbers bore me to tears, and while they are important, going through them for me takes much effort, and I do as little of it as I can and have specific times of the week when I get in my zone to deal with the numbers.

Getting Paid

I want to focus on improving some of the processes within your accounting that many businesses struggle with. We are discussing things like getting paid on time, increasing your prices and automating anything possible in this business area. Your efforts should result in higher revenue and, subsequently, profit. Bear in mind that this often only happens in a sequence.

One of the biggest issues small business owners encounter is getting paid on time. Unless you charge on the spot, the clients often don't receive the invoice, don't pay it on time or don't pay it altogether. There are many other issues, of course, but this creates a lot of inconvenience and stress. Any business owner would love not having to chase their clients for payments.

Depending on your business model, the process of taking payments can be different; however, if you are an owner-operator of a transactional business like pest control, for example, charging on the spot is the best approach.

Using systems like **Square** allows us to do this in seconds. There is a fee associated with each transaction that Square does; however, it then saves you from having to chase anyone for payments, and the money arrives in your bank the next day. Many alternatives, such as **EFTPOS** from your bank or a payment terminal from providers like Stripe, can facilitate a similar process. The idea is to keep the transactions clean and integrated with your accounting software system to avoid all the laborious invoice reconciliation later.

I recommend using proposal software if you are outside a transactional business model and charge a higher price for your product or service.

There are many benefits to doing this, but in terms of the accounting side of things, you can get the client to digitally accept your proposal, take a payment (or a deposit or even start a payment plan) using a credit card and get notified if the proposal has been opened. Not only will this supercharge your sales process, but you will be able to automate a part or all of your payment process.

If you run a repeat business model like my digital marketing agency, here are some recommendations for you to streamline your recurring payments:

1. Choose a good accounting software system with system integration (preferably native). My choice of accounting system is **Xero**.

2. Add payment methods that suit your customer. In our case, having **Stripe** for credit card payments and **GoCardless** for direct deposit works best.

3. If you conduct your business in multiple currencies, check out a system called **Airwallex** that takes care of that.

These systems easily work with repeating invoices and automate regular recurring payments. If you are worried about the transaction fees, you can add them to your invoice. You will be surprised that most people would not mention the fees to get credit card points.

With clients that have yet to pay, things can be a little more complicated, but it's not always doom and gloom. Fifty per cent of the time, people genuinely have cash flow issues and try to avoid the conversation. If this is the case, working out a payment plan with the client is the best solution. Every time I initiate this, the client has agreed to the payment plan. Let's be honest; getting paid through a payment arrangement is better than going through the letters of demand and all the legal avenues.

For some reason, however, many business owners try to conduct the uneasy debt collection process via email or SMS. Nobody wants to talk about the problem. Getting on the phone and understanding the situation, showing empathy and working out a solution is best. You won't believe the number of times the client had to speak to someone about their problems (mostly personal and unrelated to work carried out) to make their payments then.

Profit and Loss

Now let's talk about the hard stuff, your profit and loss statement. You can skip the rest of this chapter if you are a startup. A profit and loss (P&L) statement is an extremely important document for companies that offer products or services for sale. A P&L statement provides detailed insight into the financial health of a business by showing revenues, expenses, and net income or loss. Businesses need to review their P&L statements occasionally to understand where their profits are coming from and how much money is being spent on operating costs.

It would be best if you focused on some key things when reviewing your company's P&L statement. The first thing you need to do with your P&L is examining your revenues. The top line of a P&L statement shows the period's total revenue, including sales of goods and services.

Examining this number over time will help you determine if there is an upward or downward trend in revenue, which can be caused by changes in marketing, sales or simple seasonality of the business. Looking at individual revenue sources may also provide insights into which areas are most profitable and deserve more attention. If you run multiple services, set up your business revenue streams accurately to record income and expenses for each stream.

The second thing you must focus on in a P&L is understanding and controlling costs. Monitoring business costs is important as they can greatly impact profitability closely. It would help if you took the time to analyse each expense item, such as payroll costs, supplies, materials and travel-related costs. Look for opportunities to reduce costs where possible while still maintaining the quality standards of your business. Knowing the major operating expenses can help you make more informed decisions about how best to manage those costs as we advance.

Finally and most importantly, understand your profit. This is the difference between revenues and expenses. Suppose your company has been making losses consistently. In that case, it's important to closely inspect every detail of your previous years' statements to identify potential areas where improvements could be made.

It could often be a matter of poor sales processes, overall market positioning or operational changes that may set you back. Analysing overall trends in profit rather than just one specific instance often gives a better indication of whether your business model is succeeding.

In conclusion, be mindful of the importance of P&L and be able to read and interpret it. In terms of any changes or the big-picture stuff, I still recommend speaking to your accountant or financial adviser.

Choosing the Right Accountant

Having the right accountant is the key to growing your business while avoiding some unpleasant surprises, such as large tax bills. Revenue forecasting, advice on your systems, and industry benchmarking are some things your accountant should be able to help you with.

Communicating effectively with your accountant is the most important part of the accounting service. While most accountants are introverts, having regular meetings with a clear structure can help you get the best outcome. Initiate the meetings and clarify what you need and your goals.

Most accountants offer an annual meeting to forecast and review your business finances. In most situations, more is needed, as businesses can change drastically throughout the year. I recommend basing the meetings on what the most successful clients of your accountant with similar business models are doing in terms of systems, processes and goals. You may be surprised at what you learn in these meetings.

Here are some tips that will help you choose an accountant.

Firstly find a person who understands your business and the basic processes that you are involved in.

Secondly, please avoid falling for the standard suite of services they may offer. You need the absolute best and understand that your accountant can assist you when your business grows.

Thirdly, ask them about their clients and specialisation to see if this aligns with your goals or business growth objectives.

Finally, build a relationship with your accountant, so your conversations aren't just about finances. This helps to remove the tension and stress from meeting with them and keep them aware of what else is happening in your life. This is super important as many accountants focus on the business and disregard the personal side of their clients. And essentially, what you want to do is you want to make sense of it so you can make decisions based around. So yeah, Delegate focuses and cash flow use systems. And I'm sure you'll do better than you're doing right now.

Chapter Summary

1. Goals aren't just dreams but actionable roadmaps. Break down big goals into micro-goals to make them manageable and track progress.

2. Knowing both your primary and secondary personality profiles helps tailor your approach to tasks and interpersonal interactions, turning weaknesses into opportunities.

3. Create a culture of flow within your team by aligning activities with natural strengths, enhancing both performance and job satisfaction.

4. Implement the Pomodoro Technique to enhance focus and productivity. Break work into 25-minute intervals with short breaks.

5. Delegate effectively to focus on high-impact tasks that align with your strengths. Prioritise tasks based on urgency and importance using a task list.

6. **Four Key Areas of Business**:

- **Marketing: Understand the 3 Ms—Market, Media, Message—to tailor your strategy effectively.**

- **Sales: Adopt the 3 Cs—Conversation, Connection, Conversion—to refine your sales process and increase close rates.**

- **Operations: Strive for excellence and manage time efficiently to boost productivity.**

- **Accounting: Focus on getting paid promptly and regularly reviewing your profit and loss statements to ensure financial health.**

CHAPTER 5

THE PROGRAM

CHAPTER 5

THE PROGRAM

I've designed this program for busy business owners to help them improve their businesses and get better overall outcomes. Based on my experience working with my clients, I've put together this program. The program is based on making simple changes that result in more time for the owners, better clients and ultimately, more revenue.

I found that people are getting too stuck in their businesses without a clear plan to follow, where most either use their intuition or get hung up in the daily routine. The end goal of this program is to build a good business that works for you, not the other way around. In previous chapters, we discussed the importance of work-life balance and focusing on what you do to get the desired outcome.

The program I've put together is relatively straightforward but requires focus and clarity at each step. The program has four steps that need to be followed in a sequence.

1. The first step is to set goals and develop a realistic plan. The goal-setting process I follow was already covered in chapter 4.

2. The second step focuses on freeing up time to execute what you've planned in the first step. This step involves letting go, systemising processes, or hiring people to delegate tasks.

3. The third step is about fixing and improving your current processes. Identifying what needs to be fixed is the key to finding solutions that need to be put in place.

Finally, the fourth and final step is to scale. If you have a genuine business (not a job you've created for yourself), it needs to be scalable. Only then can you achieve the true potential of your business.

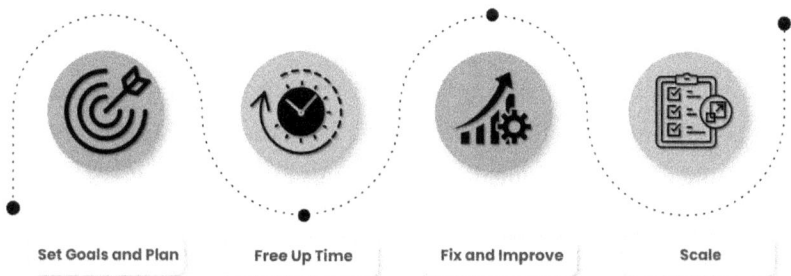

| Set Goals and Plan | Free Up Time | Fix and Improve | Scale |

Step 1: Set Goals and Plan

Setting business goals can be as straightforward or complicated as you want them to be. It's more about getting things done by setting goals instead of making them perfect. Over time the things we initially want become things we don't necessarily need. When setting goals, we often consider goals based on our state of mind. While setting goals is super important, it's equally essential to evaluate those goals over time and understand their importance. This is particularly relevant if you are setting goals independently (as opposed to having a coach). So feel free to make an extensive list of goals and refine and trim them over time.

Whatever your business goals are, it is essential to have a measurable outcome and understand what's required to reach them. For example, if your plan is hitting a higher revenue, what would your business need to do to produce this outcome? Is it improving your sales and marketing, increasing prices, hiring more people, investing in tools or a combination of these? If so, what is the easiest one you can focus on that will make the most significant difference?

It's interesting to see that every time I meet with business owners and talk to them about their goals and what needs to be done, most immediately know the answer. What needs to be added is usually the plan to reach the desired destination and/or time to do it.

Once you've defined your goals, developing a plan is your next step. I've got a framework for you to follow. The **Goal to Plan Framework** is a simple way of breaking down your goals by asking yourself the right questions. The question you need to ask yourself is, "What do I need to do in order to achieve this goal?" Then from there, you need to break the goal down into simpler micro-goals that can be broken into small tasks. Once you have defined the functions, ask yourself, "who is the best person to help me with this?" People often don't achieve goals because they involve too many activities, and they naturally get overwhelmed. Also, they try to take on each task themselves.

The Goal to Plan framework is based on breaking down your goals into micro-goals and tasks that need to be done. If the goal is to buy a house, you need to break that goal into micro-goals. The first micro goal may be saving enough money for a deposit. The second micro goal could be to find the right property, and the third could be getting finance approved. With the first micro-goal, it then comes down to a task list to achieve the desired micro-goal. In this instance, the focus should be on saving, making additional money, or thinking outside the box (for example, borrowing from family) to achieve the desired outcome.

Here is the framework:

MAIN GOAL
EG. BUY PROPERTY

	TASKS	WHO CAN HELP?
MICRO-GOAL EG. SAVE FOR DEPOSIT	SAVING PLAN ADDITIONAL INCOME BORROW MONEY	ME ALEX PARENTS
MICRO-GOAL EG. FIND THE RIGHT PROPERTY		

While some tasks may be complex or not within your comfort zone, the best thing you can do is research alternative ways to achieve your micro-goals. Rubbing shoulders with the right people and asking the right questions helps. For each task, ask yourself, "Who is the best person to help me with this? Approaching people in the realm of your micro-goals can help you discover additional avenues to reaching them.

Most people need to realise they may have more connections than initially thought. I've met business owners who have been able to change their entire sales process by learning about gap selling, a concept that they did not know was possible or could think about themselves.

Having abstract goals is another typical pattern when speaking to business owners. By abstract, I mean goals like "I want to work less" or "I want passive income". If you are stuck in something similar or thinking about these sorts of goals, ask yourself, "what does that mean in terms of outcome?" Does working less allow you to spend more time with the family or do more work on your business or do something completely different? This clarity is what people are missing to get closer to where they want to be. The lack of specificity and the goal result prevents people from creating a viable action plan.

To summarise the planning side, here are some essential things you need to consider:

1. **Base your plans on clear goals.**

2. **Set realistic deadlines and allow sufficient time for each of your dreams.**

3. **Ensure you have the right skills and resources to act on your goals or engage competent service providers.**

4. **Establish milestones or KPIs to measure yourself and focus on the results associated with these.**

Step 2: Free Up Time

The real problem for business owners is finding time to do things. You may have enthusiastically set your goals and done your planning, but the real question still stands, when are you planning to do it all? Besides, the nature of business owners would get them to use all their free time. This is because the list of tasks for business owners is usually never-ending.

The goal is to realise what is less important that you can drop, delegate or do differently.

If you are still looking for time, the best way is to go through the critical processes of your business across the four areas of the business that we covered in the previous chapter. Look for tasks that can be delegated and won't cost you an arm and a leg to outsource. Most business owners who are stuck typically end up doing everything. The biggest and the easiest thing to delegate is typically tasks like parts of your sales and marketing.

Virtual Assistants

Typically, there is particularly much time wasted in the sales process of most businesses. This may sound crazy, but let me explain. If you break this down into receiving the inquiries, qualifying them and then selling. You will quickly realise that a lot of this time could be more productive, and if you filtered the enquiries you took, you'd get a lot more done. Imagine if you could delegate the first two parts of the process.

The goal here would be to reduce the number of people you speak to through a better filtering qualifying process. What will also happen is that you'll become a lot less available, and this will instantly increase the value of prospects speaking with you after speaking to your gatekeeper.

If you are a busy business owner (which I am sure you are), having a gatekeeper in your business is necessary. I know what you are thinking! You may not be keen to get another person or may not afford them. I get this, so I recommend investing in a virtual assistant (VA).

Getting someone with excellent phone skills from the Philippines is the best and most cost-effective solution. I suggest simplifying their role so that they only focus on the enquiries and engage them for as long as you need them. They should be able to handle email, calls and social media enquiries. Don't try to get your VA to do everything for you, as they will likely fail. Finally, ensure you invest the time into training them so they understand your business and critical processes. If you are considering how to set this up, I've got this covered in the resource section of my website, **BetterBusinessThatWorks.com**.

Getting a virtual assistant is an easy way to free up 10-15 hours of your time per week. The idea is so you can now spend this time working on your business. Stay focused on trying to get more, as this will help you grow your business a little and then get stuck again. The goal is to work on your business towards your goals. I have a VA in every business that I run, and frankly, I don't know how I'd be able to run these businesses without them. This allows me to have a better focus on working towards my goals.

Systems

I often get asked, "what else can you do to free up your time in business?". Business growth comes down to two things which are people and systems. We've covered VA as an extra person who arrives at a fraction of the salary price; now, let's talk about systems.

Having a system as your business's backbone is your business's next step. Whether it's a CRM, a workflow system or a project management system, you'll need help to grow once you have over two employees. I found this out the hard way. Managing through two people becomes difficult, and productivity drops due to poor communication, multitasking and double-handling.

Here are some recommendations if you are looking for systems to implement into your business to free up time. If you have few systems in place, get everyone to start using a shared calendar. This allows you to synchronise everyone with the activities throughout the day and add notes about each activity to reduce unnecessary communication.

Once you have your calendar, the next step is implementing a project management system. This aims to get your team to follow processes and enables quality control. If you master this, you may want to look into a CRM or an ERP that would bring all your systems together.

Systems are a powerful way to supercharge your business and take it to the next level. To get your systems to work, however, you need to clearly define your processes and break them down into easy-to-understand and follow steps. Most businesses that fail at implementing systems either make their processes too complex or fail to standardise them.

In conclusion, systems will only be effective when they are being used. Unfortunately, even the best plans sometimes fail as they need to get used. If you decide to go down the path of implementing systems, please take this seriously and invest the time into team training.

Step 3: Fix and Improve

Hopefully, by now, you've freed up a few hours to work on your business and are ready to get onto the next challenge: fixing and improving your business. I often get companies enquiring about this as the first thing they want to address. Improving something without having clear goals and without any extra time can be pretty stressful. So before jumping into this, please go over your goals for what you want to achieve from this exercise.

Improving Marketing - The Top-to-Bottom Approach

If you want to fix and improve your business to make it more efficient, follow the flow through the **four areas of the business (Marketing, Sales, Operations and Accounting)**. The objective is to optimise each business area by working through the main KPIs. This improvement is really about creating quality vs chasing quantity.

With **The Top to Bottom approach**, let's start with your marketing. For example, start by reviewing the number of users visiting your website. The goal here would be to evaluate the quality of these visitors and see if you can improve this quality and then increase it. This can be complicated as your traffic often comes from various sources. I advise reviewing your controlled traffic (e.g. paid ads like **Google Ads**).

The traffic quality would define your website's final conversion goal. If your website aims to generate leads, you need to track phone calls and web form submissions. Have this set up correctly and use at least three months worth of traffic data, as specific sources might not be the primary ways to convert website visitors into enquiries; instead, they would be assisting them.

Once you've done this, move to the next part of your marketing, the website conversions and see if you can improve and increase them. If you are looking for ways to improve this, check out the resources of **BetterBusinessThatWorks.com**.

The parts of your Marketing for The Top to Bottom Approach include these areas:

- Website visitors

- Controlled traffic ads

- Traffic sources

- Website conversion rate

- Enquiry quality

If you can improve each of these areas by 10%, you will see a substantial increase in your overall Marketing outcome. If you are running an e-commerce website, you must consider other factors such as average transaction value, customer repeat buying rate and factors that may impact these.

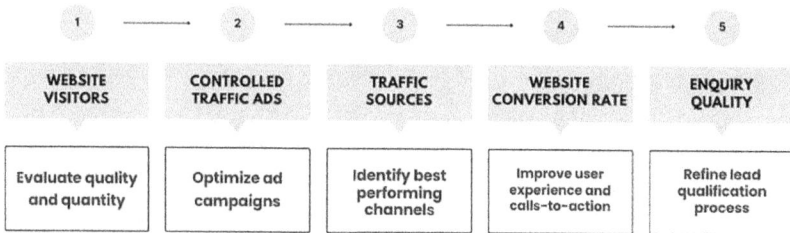

1	2	3	4	5
WEBSITE VISITORS	**CONTROLLED TRAFFIC ADS**	**TRAFFIC SOURCES**	**WEBSITE CONVERSION RATE**	**ENQUIRY QUALITY**
Evaluate quality and quantity	Optimize ad campaigns	Identify best performing channels	Improve user experience and calls-to-action	Refine lead qualification process

Holes in Your Sales Funnel

Once you've gone over marketing, the next step is to work on your sales side of the business. Most business owners are eager to apply The Top to Bottom approach to sales. If you follow this logic, however, you will naturally want to get more leads for your sales team. This is, unfortunately, a recipe for disaster as there are usually holes within the business' sales funnel.

Rather than going from top to bottom, it's best to address your sales area of the business in reverse. Analyse the clients you are converting and what brings them to a sale. Typically you will find that those clients had prior knowledge of your business (e.g. word of mouth, reviews online) before contacting you, or they had a follow-up conversation that got them over the line. Look for these patterns to see if you can identify these holes. If you want to look at this from another perspective, you are starting with the conversion rate analysis of your sales process.

To make sure we are on the same page, these are the steps of a typical sales funnel from the perspective of the business:

- Lead acquired

- Qualifying (1st and 2nd steps are often merged in digital marketing)

- Conversation

- Proposal / Quote

- Follow-up

- Sale

The follow-up step of an existing business' sales funnel makes the most significant difference in the outcome. The volume of leads often affects this as sales reps get too focused on the new information coming in rather than on the current opportunities. The follow-up, however, needs to be structured around your quote, proposal or a prior conversation that you've had; otherwise, it becomes weak. Some great reasons for a follow-up are touching base if the quote was received if it made sense if any additional information is required. Hopefully, you get the idea.

The right timing is another huge aspect of making sales. Sales reps fail to connect with them in time. Speaking to a lead when it comes in, you want to do this as soon as possible. With the quote or proposal, you need to send this out within a reasonable amount of time, depending on the nature of the service. Regarding follow-up, depending on the urgency of the service, typically, 24 hours is a reasonable amount of time to follow up on a lead.

Implementing systems in your sales funnel will save much time. I recommend investing in a system like **PandaDoc** to streamline your proposals. This will not only get them out faster but will also make them stand out. This system will also be able to notify you of the prospect's interaction with the proposal (e.g. opened and signed).

The issue with most quotes or proposals is that they often need to include more information than just the pricing. So including additional information like your guarantees, points of difference (e.g. why choose us), and information on past projects (case studies) reinforces the message.

Using a CRM for your sales is a huge benefit, especially if you have multiple team members. The CRM allows you to store all the contact information, past interactions, and a log of marketing assets with which the contact would have interacted. In addition, CRM allows you to set up automation to create lead follow-ups, which can help you free up time. Use your CRM if you've got it.

LEAD ACQUIRED

QUALIFYING

CONVERSATION

PROPOSAL QUOTE

FOLLOW-UP

SALE

People, Systems and Processes

When it comes to what your business does (the core of your business, let's call this "the core"), you have to be good at what you do. This book is about something other than helping you better in your trade, and the focus is instead looking at this as operations. The operations part of your business is made up of the core, people, systems and processes. The goal of improving the operations side of your business is to create a smooth flow.

Let's start looking into improving your operations by addressing you and your team, the people side of your business. Every person who joins your business brings their own background and working style, and if you are happily running a small team, the easiest thing to do is to create systems and processes around that person. For example, getting them to use the tools and templates they are good with. This would allow you to enable flow very quickly; the issue, however, is scalability. If you are getting new team members onboard, then it may become difficult to do this for every person. This is why large organisations create systems and processes and get people to follow them. This depends on your goals and growth appetite.

The size of your team directly impacts the productivity of your business. The team will typically be more productive if you've addressed your systems and processes. However, the growth of the business requires adjusting these processes based on the change in the business. Poor systems and processes lead to consistent results and a drop in productivity. For every person you are onboarding without a set structure, you will drop 10-30% in productivity. So be careful before you start scaling things up.

Finding the right people for your business is a dream for every business. Earlier in this book, we discussed Wealth Dynamics, Personality Profiling and creating flow through synergy. I advise you to profile each promising-looking candidate before you offer them a position. Put people on a probationary period before they become permanent. Ensure your new staff members are good at the core of your business but can also sync with the rest of your team. The last thing you want is conflicts and toxicity, which create stress and take much time to resolve.

Team culture is another topic you need to consider for a business, and it must be addressed in many small businesses. Team culture is all about the vibe or environment you have at your work, which connects your team's personal and professional sides. You might have some people professionally a lot more experienced than my senior and what they do with other people; however, when it comes to the social side of things, it could be the other way around; the whole idea is to have socially everyone aligned around interests.

Here are some examples of activities that create a good team culture. Daily morning check-in calls allow everyone to sync and be aware of what everyone else is doing. Doing weekly events like Beer O'clock allows everyone to sync. Doing things like a monthly development meeting helps team members share their goals and struggles and allows you, as the business leader, to address these problems. Getting your team to feel the support you and other team members provide is crucial. You would be surprised, but sometimes simple things like buying a car may create stress for your team members. So in terms of team culture, make it fun, but also try to identify areas where you or other team members can help each other. Setting goals and getting team members to participate in the foundation of business team culture.

Using Systems

We've already covered using systems in previous chapters, and this should be no exception when it comes to operations. Standardising and centralising your operations through a plan and set processes avoids confusion and reduces mistakes. Run regular training for your team to make sure they are efficient at following the systems you've got.

Having a system in your business sounds like a dream by now; however, systems don't work without well-defined processes. With many systems you are implementing, you are inheriting the operations as a part of that system. If that works for your business, that's great; however, if not, this is where you need to work on your business processes.

Many business owners need help with processes, especially in newly established businesses. If you are finding that each client is different and requires special treatment or a tailored approach, this is the bottleneck of growth. You won't be able to apply a system to a situation like this as you won't have set processes. These processes are a set of algorithms that allow you and your team to deliver the same level of quality in each job.

Here are some basic processes you must consider defining, even if they seem obvious.

- Client onboarding

- Preparation / Job setting

- Steps to carry out work

- Finishing up the job

- Communicating with related parties

Now with systems and people, once you align everything, it's about growth. Now one of the big things is that business owners tend to micromanage; even though you have a system, you always need to check up on things when you have a dedicated person. This is quite normal but counterproductive, resulting in inefficiency and double handling.

You'll always find something to improve. You'll always get something to do to pick on, and it'll never be 100%. Besides, as a business owner, you'll always think that you will always do it better. Especially if you have hands-on knowledge, the key to growth is to let go and, most importantly, coach staff to work independently and take responsibility.

Staff Coaching

Adopting a different approach to communication is essential to effectively coach your staff. Rather than simply telling your team what to do, it is more powerful to guide them towards the desired outcome using their logic and problem-solving skills. This approach was highlighted to me during an event at Google, where I learned from Revel Gordon, a coach from Sydney. The key to this approach is to ask questions encouraging your team to think for themselves and arrive at solutions.

For example, if a team member comes to you with a problem, instead of immediately providing a solution, ask them what other approaches they think could be tried. Then continue to ask follow-up questions to help guide them towards a solution. By doing so, they will arrive at a solution they are confident in and develop the ability to tackle similar problems in the future.

This approach may seem simple, but it is an effective way to encourage your team to take ownership of their work and develop their problem-solving skills. By allowing them to find their solutions, they will be better equipped to handle similar challenges in the future and become more self-sufficient. Not only will this take the burden off your hands, but it will also foster an environment of growth and development within your team.

Once you implement all the systems and train the people within your company, and you feel comfortable with how your services are delivered and look, typically, it's a good idea to reach out to your customers to find out. You know how everything's going to get some feedback is typically a good time to start scaling. Everything I look at scaling can be about something other than getting more customers. Doing things like price increases or potentially revisiting your customers to identify new opportunities could be a matter.

You'll find that you always miss something when you work with a customer. And we find that often you can solve those problems or find somebody who can solve those problems to get a better outcome. You're working with a client to work on a results-based activity. So whether engaging it to build a deck, engaging it to do a marketing campaign, or whether it be engaging you to clean your house, it's the same thing. There's got to be some tangible outcome in the end that someone can evaluate. And if that's the case, you should always seek new opportunities.

Partnering

Partnering with other companies in your industry can be a smart strategy for business growth. The key is to specialise in a niche service and deliver exceptional results. By establishing yourself as a leader in your area of expertise, you can attract the attention of potential competitors and industry peers interested in collaborating with you on complementary projects.

Feel free to start conversations and let others know about your specialised services. Recognise that you can only excel at some things, and it's better to focus on your strengths and partner with others to deliver the best possible results for your customers. This applies to all businesses, not just agencies. For example, a plumbing business may have a particular speciality that they enjoy and are profitable in. By focusing on that niche, they can attract their ideal customers and achieve better results.

Remember, the 80/20 rule applies here. Focus on what you do best and partner with others to fill the gaps. By specialising in a niche and partnering with other businesses, you can differentiate yourself from the competition, attract more clients, and, ultimately, grow your business.

Summary

There are several key steps you can take to improve your business. First, improve your current processes to ensure they are as efficient and effective as possible. Then, prioritise sales to improve your cash flow. You can also enhance your marketing efforts to attract the right kind of work for your business. To increase the transaction value, consider strategic selling and implementing upsells. Systemise or simplify your processes wherever possible to streamline operations. Finally, be prepared to scale your business as you grow and succeed. While there are many other ways to improve your business, following the above methodology works based on my experience. This process has been proven through working with various business models and individuals.

Step 4: Scale

Now, this is the final step in my program. I'm touching on the whole program to make things a little bit easier for you to understand as to what the program is all about, hopefully giving you just enough information to be aware of what you need to be doing. Scaling is quite a natural process when everything is aligned. However, not everyone is ready to scale, creating additional work and stress.

Scaling is all about ensuring enough people in the business who can deliver on your vision and that its core serves its customers. You can carry on with your goals and diminish your vision to keep your team inspired, motivated and educated, and all this has to align with the business's profit goal.

Many businesses scale naturally without much effort once all the people, systems, and processes are in place. However, others feel like they hit the ceiling where there is often little room for growth if you've fixed and improved everything. If this is the case, you are either in a very small niche with many external constraints or need to review your vision, as this may need to be aligned with growth in the first place.

If you are struggling with a way to scale your business, you should look at this from an exit strategy perspective. What is your exit plan, and what are your options? You may be thinking of turning your business into a chain or a franchise, or you want to look at selling the business. While there are many exit strategies for a business, it's the thinking that helps with a scaling plan. You'll know that to turn your business into a franchise, your processes have to be smooth and independent of you. This exercise will help you realise possible gaps and limitations of your business model.

To conclude this chapter, please be mindful and realistic that everything has a limit. You can get the best people in the world only soon to realise that taking more responsibility and growing may only be for some, or they want to stop at a certain level. You can systemise all you want only to realise that your systems will start to fail on a large scale and need to be replaced. This is why I think it's important for a business owner to realise and understand what their "sweet spot" is.

What is this "Sweet spot"? In my opinion, the "sweet spot" is simply a period in your business where everything works while allowing the business owner to work on their personal goals. This is, of course, very individual for every business owner. While some can achieve this fast and live a balanced life, others will chase buying properties, getting their kids into the best schools and so on. Neither is right nor wrong. This could be a good flight altitude for your business that adds meaning to what you do.

Chapter Summary

1. **The Goal to Plan Framework transforms abstract aspirations into actionable steps.**

2. **Virtual assistants can be a cost-effective first step in breaking the self-employment trap.**

3. **Implement systems carefully, ensuring proper training and adoption by your team.**

4. **The "Top-to-Bottom" approach in marketing prevents wasting resources on poor-quality leads.**

5. **Analyse and fix "holes" in your sales funnel, particularly in the follow-up stage.**

CHAPTER 6

QUICK WINS

CHAPTER 6

QUICK WINS

When a business realises it's time to change, it can almost be too late. Especially when it comes to marketing or sales, most of the enquiries are based on conversations like, "I need help right now". On the one hand, this makes sense; on the other hand, things shouldn't become critical for them to change. This differentiates good businesses from those where things are all over the place. Luckily, something can always be done to improve the situation; however, timing can be your worst enemy and needs to be considered.

This chapter is based on my learnings, research, and the coaching I've done over the years that allowed me to improve significantly in each business area. Sharing this with you may help you in one or many business areas. My entire approach is structured around the principle of being able to drill down on where the actual problem is. I've developed a framework based on this approach, which is based around stages as questions to ask yourself. These questions are why, what, who, how and when. Ask those questions about any task in that specific sequence to get better clarity and outcome. I've named this framework "the winning framework".

Here is an example of this framework around email marketing. Naturally, people jump into the execution part, which revolves around the "how" question. The "how" stage is more about the actual process. Unless you're an expert in email marketing or have some prior experience, it can be challenging to get a good result immediately. What's considered good?

If you apply the framework and start with the "why" question, the objectives and the process suddenly become much more straightforward. If, with an email marketing campaign, the idea is to generate sales through past customers, then it's easier to come up with the theme and content of the email.

This also allows you to identify some tasks (or the "what") that must be done. At this stage, if using technology is your challenge, you could at least provide a straightforward task and engage someone (the "who") that can help or point you in the right direction regarding the tools to use. Or hiring a content writer may be the next step once you have defined the theme of the email but can only partially write the level of content required.

Finally, then it's a matter of the "how" (the execution) and timing (the "when"). This example helps you see the process from a clearer perspective.

Some may think about the winning framework as common sense, and it's more about taking a task from beginning to end while being clear about each part of the process. This allows you to see where you may have failed and identify alternative approaches. I apply this framework to identify and execute opportunities to make quick wins. See if you can use this framework to get better results in all the critical areas of your business.

Getting More Clients

One of the most common questions we get from clients is, "can we get more leads?" While this is quite a natural question, this often is not the problem that the business needs to address. The previous chapter covered evaluating and improving your sales before jumping onto marketing. However, if you are confident that the sales side of things is under control, you've got to understand some marketing basics before starting to change things up.

While there are many ways to look at marketing, let's break it down into inbound marketing, outbound marketing, and networking. Each one of these angles of marketing has specific processes that can either be delegated or must be executed by someone with higher authority. Understanding marketing from these three angles helps you diversify your activities and understand what works best.

Inbound Marketing

Let's look into inbound marketing first. Most companies look at this most common marketing angle when starting. This is all about your business being found. Usually, inbound marketing is delivered through Search Engine Optimisation, directories or pay-per-click. Having a consistent brand and marketing message makes this work. For example, a consistent brand, your unique selling point, a call to action (e.g. Get Free Quote) and contact information. Inbound marketing becomes somewhat passive once set up and can often be outsourced, which is a considerable advantage to the business.

The best way to start with inbound marketing is by using pay-per-click advertising (e.g. **Google Ads**). Make your campaigns as specific as possible regarding your target location, time and audiences. Also, remember to apply the **ACUA principle** to your ads that we covered in earlier chapters. Inbound marketing may be costly, but it works, and it's a matter of working out if you can keep it profitable for your business. The only real challenge is doing inbound marketing for B2B (business to business) types of businesses, and this is mainly because of the passive customer journey of the prospects.

Let's go through some practical examples of the ACUA principle.

ACUA stands for Availability, Convenience, Utility and Availability. Including those factors within your ad copy or marketing material really allows you to address all the customer wants.

Let's start with Availability as one of the most significant factors.
This is because people often want something right now and are even prepared to pay more based on this. For example, with our domestic cleaning client, the number of calls we get on a Friday afternoon is enormous. Most people want cleaning done the following morning and are willing to pay more.

The next ACUA point is Convenience. How convenient do you do your service for the customer?
The best example I can give you is one of our builder clients that send their clients to Bali for a holiday while renovating. This creates convenience for the customer and is a huge selling point. Small things like free parking, especially if you're somewhere in a busy city area, add much convenience for certain types of clients.

Utility is the third point of the ACUA principle.
Why should people choose your business as opposed to somebody else? Is it your experience or awards your business has? Or supporting an organisation or being a member of an industry association may give you more credibility. This is what utility is all about.

The final part of ACUA is Affordability.

The main reason why I've put them in this sequence is that many people are tempted to jump into the "price" conversation when it should be the last thing to talk about. The affordability ensures your product is affordable and suits the customer's financial circumstances. This could be payment plans, accepting credit cards, or having options like AfterPay. Don't confuse affordable and cheap.

When it comes to inbound marketing, the key is doing it. It's a matter of running campaigns, finetuning your conversion rates and adjusting parts of your campaigns (e.g. ads, keywords, landing pages and bidding settings) to make it work. Many startups get burned here as almost everyone tries to do inbound marketing themselves. Google also encourages this; however, the consequences are that people waste hundreds and even thousands of dollars with little return. I recommend contacting local agencies to see if they can help you with this.

Outbound Marketing

Outbound marketing is an active form of marketing that requires strategy and persistence. The activities of outbound marketing are things like cold calling, direct mail, flyer drops and events. The idea is to deliver a message to your target audience unaware of you and qualify them to activate interest.

Many businesses don't know where to start or only do what everyone else does. This is why we end up with a million spam emails from service providers (mainly marketing). To get the most out of outbound marketing, you need three things: a good quality list (names, phone numbers, email addresses), a clever message (to start the conversation), putting in the time (invest the time to get the result and keep going after getting rejected).

The overall outbound marketing strategy looks like this. Firstly, build a good list (I recommend outsourcing this part). Secondly, send out an email blast to this list with a link in the email (this allows you to qualify for interest). Finally, get on the phone and call people who have responded to your email, those who have opened the link in your email, and those who opened the email. This gives you a list of people who are most aware of your message/offer.

Business Networking

The third area is networking, about meeting other business owners and potentially joining partnerships to create strategic alliances and get referrals. This is the most potent area for most businesses, and this is the one that's overlooked the most. There's a basic concept that you can implement, which is based on finding people who have got your customers before you and are not in competition with you.

Many business networking groups are a great way to get into networking. Organisations like **"BNI"** and the **"Chamber of Commerce"** have a format that is easy to follow, allowing you to build rapport and alliances with other businesses. The key is identifying the right businesses and people to help your business grow. Then make sure to understand their businesses, educate them about yours and connect with them regularly.

Building business alliances with other businesses that complement your services can take your business to another level. As a service provider, you can only offer clients some services. Having a network of people within your industry helps deliver more solutions and have other experts working alongside you.

With our marketing, for example, many accountants and business coaches have customers asking for marketing or ways to improve cash flow and partnering with those businesses creates a logical strategic alliance. You need to know how to nurture this relationship, but the work that this avenue brings is worth the time and effort.

Strategic alliances work well when you understand the needs of the customer. If the customer journey for marketing starts with, let's say, a business coach advising as to what they need to do, then you need to partner up with those business coaches. Ideally, you want them to have more input into your business rather than just charging you for a standard service. The same would go for accountants, lawyers and other professional services that can help your business succeed.

If you can make some quick wins in your marketing, this should help you fill the gaps in your sales pipeline. Please focus on the quick wins, as ideally, you need to review your entire sales funnel and allocate the necessary resources to finetune it. The above tips inform you of what can immediately impact your current situation.

Tips to Increase Your Sales

People rarely think about sales. More naturally, people want to jump into marketing and increase leads. However, a few things can increase your revenue by finetuning the sales side of things. To do this, you have to understand the entire sales process. Once the enquiry comes in, you must know where it came from. Imagine if you could qualify that enquiry further by obtaining additional information which would help you do better in sales. Lead qualifying is the bridge between your marketing and sales.

The lead-qualifying process can be done in several ways. You can add additional form fields to your enquiry web form. Alternatively, you can get a VA or an answering service that would qualify each enquiry further before you or your sales team speak to them. For example, we found that for businesses like builders, it's essential to understand things like when someone needs the job to be done, where they are building and the project budget they have in mind. The spectrum of queries can range from a simple bathroom renovation to a new custom-built home. Addressing each enquiry in the same way, doesn't work.

Let's over-qualifying as a process and how it can help you increase revenue. The conversation around qualifying is a big part of the sales process and the information you can obtain. So let's look at the process of qualifying that I like to call 3Cs. There are three parts to a sale: there's a connection, there's a conversation, and there's a conversion. The connection is about finding the common tongue based on topics where you can establish common ground. Think about this as finding common ground to build your conversation on. This often happens when people discuss the weather, news, sport and other everyday topics.

The next part of the qualifying conversation is the conversation. This is more about the product or service; the key here is asking questions. Asking questions allows you to identify the real motivation behind the actual process. If you've heard about the gap selling approach, asking questions will enable you to determine the gaps on which to base your sale. Now, behind each gap, many pain points are the ones that the customer wants to resolve.

Your objective with qualifying is to find out the motivation and gaps. For example, if somebody is enquiring about renovations, typically, there is an entirely different motivation behind the actual need for this service. For instance, if a family is looking for more space due to the arrival of their baby. Straight away, you would know that a time constraint is attached to this. Another example would be that people want to rent their property out and maximise their rental income. This would allow you to understand the value and outcome of their investment into renovations.

Once you obtain all the necessary information and run through the **3 C's**, finalising the sale with a robust proposal is time. This is the one part, particularly in the service industry, it could have done better. A tailored recommendation based on your qualifying parameters and the customer wants to be laid out professionally with supportive information helps you get a positive outcome. Increase your prices by at least 10% with a suitable proposal as it will stand apart from the competition.

Taking Operations to Another Level

Improving your operations is critical to taking your business to the next level. There are many ways to approach this, but one of the most vital aspects is building a solid team culture. When you have staff working for you, it's crucial to understand why they're working with you and what motivates them. Building strong relationships with your team members will create a more positive work environment, boost morale, and encourage teamwork.

One way to build a strong team culture is to have regular catch-ups with your team. These meetings should go beyond work and focus on understanding your team members' goals, aspirations, and concerns. By showing an interest in your team members' lives, you'll build stronger connections and create a more supportive work environment. In his book **"The 5 Love Languages,"** Gary Chapman explores how people perceive love and appreciation differently. Whether through touch, words of affirmation, gifts, quality time, or acts of service, there are other ways to show appreciation and build relationships with your team members.

Personality profiles are another critical aspect of team building. Wealth Dynamics is a powerful concept that helps business owners identify the strengths and weaknesses of their team members. By understanding the strengths and weaknesses of each team member, you can assign tasks that align with their strengths and minimise their weaknesses. This will help create a more efficient and effective team and improve business operations.

Finally, it's essential to cultivate a positive work culture that encourages teamwork, open communication, and mutual respect. Creating a supportive work environment will foster a sense of loyalty and commitment among your team members, leading to increased job satisfaction and productivity.

Improving your business operations can be challenging, but focusing on team building, work relationships, and team culture can significantly impact your business's success. So, take the time to invest in your team, cultivate a positive work environment, and watch your business thrive.

Ways of Improving Your Cash Flow

Cash flow is the lifeblood of any business, and it determines a company's financial health and growth. Therefore, improving cash flow should be a top priority for any business owner. This chapter will explore various ways to improve cash flow and share some quick wins that have worked for our clients.

Affordability Principle

Understanding the affordability principle is crucial in determining what's possible for your business. Knowing your clients' financial capability and what they're willing to pay will help you set reasonable prices for your services, and this will ensure that you get paid on time and in full.

Credit Cards Payments

Credit card payments are an effective way to motivate customers to pay on time. Many credit cards offer rewards and points that customers can use, encouraging them to choose this payment option. Businesses can offer credit card payments and streamline payment processing by adding payment gateway systems like Stripe to accounting systems like Xero. This quick win can improve your cash flow by making it easier and more convenient for customers to pay.

Repeat Payments

For businesses with a repeat business model, setting up repeat payments through systems like Xero and Stripe can save time and ensure regular payments. This will help reduce the time spent processing fees and provide a steady cash flow.

Upfront Payment

Upfront payment is a powerful way to qualify customers more interested in your services. This quick win ensures you receive payment before starting work, minimising the risk of bad debt. You can also set up instalment payments to make it easier for customers to pay over time.

Increase Prices

Increasing prices may seem daunting, but it is the simplest way to increase cash flow. Businesses need to understand the extra value they add to their services from the customers' perspective. Proposal systems like PandaDoc can help enterprises show their worth by including "Why to Choose Us," team profiles, insurance, and methodology. This quick win can help businesses deliver value and increase prices without losing customers.

Debt Collection

Debt collection can significantly impact cash flow. Taking upfront payments, setting up instalments, and having a good relationship with clients can help minimise the risk of bad debt. This quick win ensures that businesses get paid on time and in full. In conclusion, improving cash flow is crucial for any business. The quick wins discussed in this chapter can help businesses streamline payment processing, ensure they get paid on time, and reduce bad debt. By implementing these strategies, businesses can improve their financial health and ensure growth.

Chapter Summary

1. **The ACUA principle (Availability, Convenience, Utility, Affordability) transforms generic services into compelling propositions.**

2. **Inbound marketing for B2B can be challenging due to the passive customer journey.**

3. **Qualify leads by understanding motivation and gaps, not just collecting basic information.**

4. **Upfront payments improve cash flow and help qualify serious clients.**

5. **Use personality profiling in hiring to create a diverse, complementary team.**

CHAPTER 7

THE BIG PICTURE

CHAPTER 7

THE BIG PICTURE

Running a small business can be a highly rewarding experience. You can turn your passion into a career, create something meaningful, and make a difference in your community. However, it can also be a challenging endeavour that requires a deep understanding of what it takes to succeed. In this chapter, we'll explore the big picture behind running a small business and why it's essential not to micromanage but instead focus on quality and growth.

Your Role

As the owner of a small business, your role is multifaceted. You're responsible for everything from creating a business plan to hiring employees, managing finances, and building customer relationships. To be successful, you need to have a clear understanding of what you're trying to achieve and how you're going to get there. This will change throughout your business journey, so review your goals and adjust your processes accordingly.

One of small business owners' most significant challenges is knowing when to step back and let others take the reins. Many entrepreneurs are highly driven and passionate individuals who are used to being in control. However, this approach can be counterproductive when trying to run a successful small business.

Micromanaging is a common mistake that many small business owners make. It's understandable to want to keep a close eye on everything happening within your business, but micromanaging can stifle creativity, productivity, and growth. When you micromanage, you're telling your employees you don't trust them to do their jobs effectively. This lack of trust can demoralise your team, leading to low morale and poor performance.

To avoid micromanaging, hiring the right people and providing them with the tools and resources they need to succeed is crucial. Trust your team to do their jobs and focus on providing guidance and support when needed. As a small business owner, your role should be to create a vision for your company, set clear expectations, and let your team get to work.

Quality is essential when running a successful small business, and it sets you apart from your competitors and keeps customers coming back. However, maintaining high-quality standards can take time and effort, especially when growing your business. To maintain quality, it's essential to clearly understand what your customers want and expect. Conduct market research and gather feedback from your customers regularly. Use this information to make necessary improvements and adjustments to your products or services.

Investing in quality also means investing in your employees. Providing ongoing training and development opportunities can help your team stay up-to-date with your industry's latest trends and best practices. This investment can pay off in the long run, leading to higher-quality products and services and increased customer loyalty.

Finally, growth is a critical component of running a successful small business. Without growth, your business may stagnate, losing competitiveness in your market. A growth mindset is essential to achieving and sustaining growth in a business. This means taking risks, trying new things, and exploring new opportunities. It also means clearly understanding your target market and how to reach them.

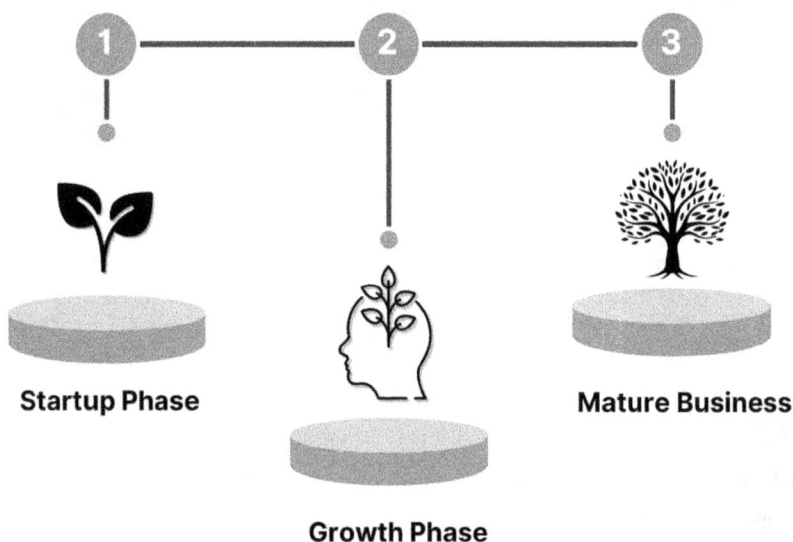

Startup Phase

Growth Phase

Mature Business

What's Next?

You are about to or have already built a business from the ground up, but what's next? It's time to think about sharing your knowledge, running another, more leveraged business through e-commerce, and investing in your future.

After building a successful business, you have a wealth of knowledge and expertise that others can benefit from. You can share your knowledge through speaking engagements, mentoring, coaching, or writing a book.

SHARING
KNOWLEDGE

E-COMMERCE
EXPANSION

WHAT'S NEXT?

PERSONAL
DEVELOPMENT

INVESTING FOR
THE FUTURE

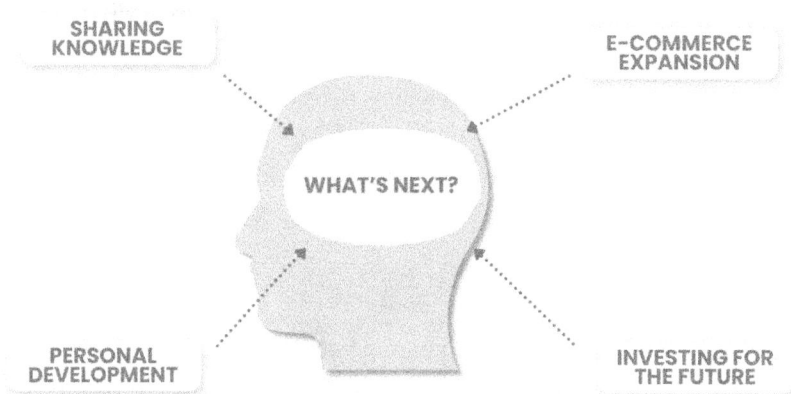

Mentoring and Coaching

You can share your knowledge by mentoring or coaching others. Look for aspiring entrepreneurs who could benefit from your guidance, and offer to help them get started. You can also provide coaching services to business owners who want to take their businesses to the next level.

Writing a book: Writing a book is another excellent way to share your knowledge and establish yourself as an expert. Your book could focus on your area of expertise, your entrepreneurial journey, or lessons learned from building a successful business.

Expanding your business through e-commerce is an excellent way to reach a wider audience and increase revenue. E-commerce offers many advantages, such as increased visibility, reduced overhead costs, and the ability to sell to customers worldwide.

To start with e-commerce, you must create an online store. Many platforms make it easy to set up and manage an online store. Choose a venue that meets your needs and offers the necessary features to succeed.

Investing your money is an integral part of securing your financial future. After building a successful business, you may have extra funds to invest in creating additional income streams.

Many investment options are available, including stocks, bonds, real estate, and more. Research and choose investments that align with your goals and risk tolerance.

Investing in yourself by continuing to learn and develop new skills is also essential. Attend events, take courses, read books and listen to podcasts on topics that interest you. This will help you stay current with industry trends and prepare for future opportunities.

Online Store Projects and Why You Should Invest in One

In today's rapidly changing business landscape, online stores are becoming increasingly popular for entrepreneurs and established businesses. With lower overhead costs, greater flexibility, and the ability to reach a global audience, online stores offer several advantages over the traditional physical store model. This chapter will explore the benefits of running an online store compared to a physical store.

Lower Overhead Costs

One of the most significant advantages of running an online store is the lower overhead costs. Unlike physical stores, online stores do not require investment in rent associated with a physical location. This reduced cost structure allows businesses to operate with lower overhead costs and potentially higher profit margins.

Increased Reach

Online stores can reach a global audience without being limited by geographic location or foot traffic. This allows businesses to access a larger customer base and potentially increase sales. Additionally, online stores can operate 24/7, allowing customers to shop whenever it is convenient for them, leading to increased customer satisfaction and loyalty.

Greater Flexibility

Online stores offer greater flexibility compared to physical stores. For example, online stores can be easily scaled up or down to meet changing customer demand, without the need for additional physical space or resources. Additionally, online stores can offer a wider range of products or services without the limitations of physical space.

Easier to Track and Analyse Data

Online stores offer access to valuable customer data and analytics, which can be used to make data-driven decisions and optimise the customer experience. This can include data on customer behaviour, preferences, and demographics, allowing businesses to tailor their offerings and marketing strategies accordingly.

Lower Marketing Costs

Online stores can often be marketed more cost-effectively than traditional stores through channels such as social media and email marketing. This can lead to lower marketing costs and a higher return on investment (ROI).

Reduced Risk of Theft or Damage

Online stores do not have to worry about physical theft or damage to inventory, reducing the risk of financial loss. This can also lead to reduced insurance costs for businesses.

In conclusion, running an online store offers several advantages over the traditional physical store model, including lower overhead costs, increased reach, greater flexibility, easier data tracking and analysis, lower marketing costs, and reduced risk of theft or damage. By embracing the online store model, businesses can unlock new opportunities for growth, profitability, and success in today's dynamic marketplace.

KEY FACTORS	Online Store	Physical Store
Overhead Costs	Lower overhead costs (no rent, utilities)	▲ Higher overhead costs (rent, utilities, staff)
Customer Reach	Global customer base	▲ Limited to local customers
Flexibility	Operates 24/7 Easy inventory updates	▲ Limited operating hours ▲ Physical space constraints
Data Analytics	Detailed customer data access	▲ Limited data collection
Marketing Costs	Lower digital marketing costs	▲ Higher costs for physical advertising
Risk of Theft/ Damage	Lower risk (secure payments, digital goods)	▲ Higher risk of theft and damage to inventory

Legacy

This book discusses the importance of building a sustainable business that can last for the long term. It is crucial to understand that business is more like a marathon than a sprint, and there will be changes along the way. We have emphasised the need to focus on the long-term return rather than rushing for quick outcomes.

Every business is different, and it is essential to understand that every business is about the business owner fulfilling their dreams and vision while ensuring that the people who work for them can solve problems and fulfil that vision.

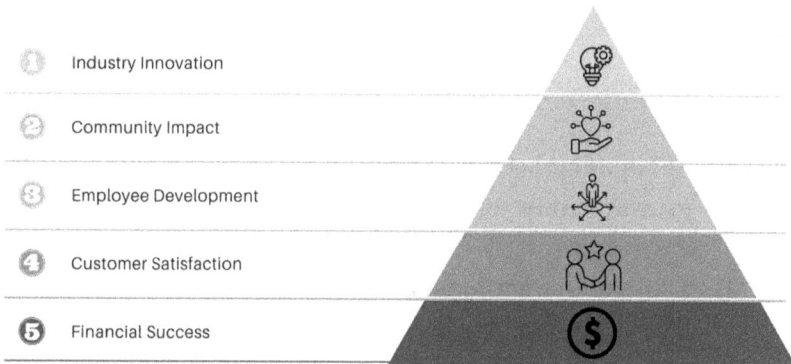

1	Industry Innovation
2	Community Impact
3	Employee Development
4	Customer Satisfaction
5	Financial Success

Do a reality check with your business now and again. Do this from the point of the business model perspective, the types of clients you work with and the money you get paid for the services you provide. Many business owners need help to let go, only to get stuck in the self-employed cycle and never make it to a good business. The best way to understand this is by going over the Cashflow Quadrant concept by Robert Kiyosaki. Once you know the idea, it's really about getting the right people to join your team, putting systems in place and letting go.

Once you have your business working, asking yourself what's next is crucial. Will you reinvest your cash flow into your business, or is there something else you want to do with your free time and resources? We have recommended looking into Roger Hamilton's legacy concept to explore what legacy you want to leave behind.

To help you further, we have created a Resources section for this book on my website, including my coaching program, an online version, and other tools and recommendations for your business.

In conclusion, we hope the ideas and concepts discussed in this book have been valuable and insightful. Remember, running a business requires a business mindset and a long-term perspective. Keep building, keep growing, and keep learning.

Chapter Summary

1. **Avoid micromanagement to foster creativity and growth within your team.**

2. **E-commerce isn't just about selling online; it's about leveraging data for personalised experiences.**

3. **Writing a book can be a powerful tool for refining and sharing your business philosophy.**

4. **Online stores excel in reach and the ability to rapidly test and iterate business models.**

5. **Your business legacy is shaped more by the problems you solve than by profit alone.**

BONUS CHAPTER

AFTERMATH

BONUS CHAPTER

AFTERMATH

Since I penned the first draft of Better Business That Works, the landscape of my professional life has changed dramatically. Initially, I was caught in the whirlwind of perfecting the text and adding substantive content. However, as I navigated the complexities of operating three distinct businesses amidst shifting markets, I realised that the chaos of change was not a disruptor but a doorway to new opportunities.

The evolution of the market brought a surge of inquiries from B2B businesses. These enterprises were eager yet unsure how to seize the emerging opportunities. This influx led me to question the relevance of my original manuscript.

Had the business environment evolved so drastically that my eighteen years of experience was no longer applicable? It seemed, ironically, that I was falling out of love with the very business practices I had advocated for others to fall back in love with.

Embracing Change in Business Evolution

Change is inevitable in business, and sometimes it comes in waves that threaten to overwhelm us. I've always preached about adaptability, but now I was being tested on my own principles. The fundamental question became: Do I abandon what I know and leap into the unknown, or do I leverage my established expertise in new ways?

This is a crossroads many business owners face. When markets shift and client demands evolve, there's often a temptation to completely reinvent your business model. However, what I discovered was that the core principles of effective business remain constant—it's the application that needs adjustment.

Reconnecting Through Experience

Instead of plunging into unfamiliar territories, I turned to my past—a portfolio of clients with whom I'd built strong, trusting relationships. One such relationship was with Jo Burgess, co-founder of **Shortcuts Software**. I introduced her to a new methodology I had developed, tailored specifically for businesses looking to reinvent their B2B strategies. This methodology was not just theoretical but a tested approach refined through the lens of practical, hands-on application and tailored to the needs of the modern market.

By focusing on what I was naturally good at—building relationships and developing strategic visions—I was able to bring fresh value to existing connections rather than starting from scratch.

Crafting a Roadmap for Success

My collaboration with Shortcuts Software began with a series of strategic meetings aimed at crafting a comprehensive marketing roadmap. The process was spearheaded by Artur, their adept Marketing Manager, and spanned three intensive weeks.

The approach I developed reflects the systematic thinking I've advocated throughout this book. Just as the 80/20 principle helps identify what truly matters, this structured approach helped Shortcuts Software identify their most valuable opportunities and crucial challenges.

First Meeting: Current Strategy and Gap Analysis

In our initial session, we dissected Shortcuts' existing strategies to pinpoint inefficiencies and gaps. We reviewed their ongoing activities, revealing several disconnects between what they were doing and what they wanted to achieve. Their product positioning was solid, but market placement needed refinement. Their digital assets weren't being leveraged effectively, and their website wasn't performing to its potential.

Their marketing campaigns were tracking metrics that didn't translate to business growth, and their sales approach had too many touchpoints creating confusion rather than clarity. Most importantly, we identified unique points of differentiation from competitors—aspects they hadn't capitalised on in their marketing. This whole process exemplifies the importance of honest assessment. Without this clarity, you're essentially navigating without a compass.

Second Meeting: Market Trends, Competitors, and Opportunities

With our internal assessment complete, we shifted focus to external factors. We conducted a thorough competitor analysis, examining not just who their competitors were, but what made them successful. This revealed several market gaps that Shortcuts could strategically fill. We explored new marketing channels they hadn't fully utilised and projected their potential impacts on lead generation.

The market was changing rapidly, with salon and spa owners becoming increasingly tech-savvy. We studied these trends to position Shortcuts ahead of the curve rather than chasing it. We identified low-hanging fruit—opportunities for immediate action—and strategies to re-engage past clients who had fallen silent.

We discussed specific client challenges in depth, from onboarding friction to retention issues, and developed engagement techniques tailored to different audience segments. By understanding where the valuable opportunities lie and focusing resources effectively, businesses can achieve significant results without spreading themselves too thin.

Third Meeting: Marketing Roadmap and Actionable Plan

Our analysis culminated in an actionable marketing roadmap—not just theory, but a practical implementation plan. We highlighted quick wins for immediate implementation, including optimising their Google Business Profile and restructuring email sequences to better nurture leads.

We designed scalable marketing processes for sustainable growth, creating templates and workflows that could be repeated and refined over time. Mapping the complete customer journey revealed several points where potential clients were falling through the cracks.

With this understanding, we developed a comprehensive omni-channel strategy with consistent yet tailored messaging for each platform. We focused on cross-channel engagement, creating a cohesive experience guiding prospects toward becoming clients regardless of where they first encountered the brand.

By creating clear processes with defined responsibilities, Shortcuts could now scale their marketing efforts without being dependent on any single person—building a business rather than just creating another job.

From Implementation to Transformation

The real power of a strategic roadmap isn't just in its creation—it's in the implementation. With Shortcuts Software, we didn't simply deliver a document without follow-up. We established accountability measures, key performance indicators, and regular check-in points to ensure the plan transformed from theory to practice.

This is where many businesses falter. They create impressive strategies that collect dust on digital shelves. The difference between a business that stagnates and one that thrives often comes down to execution discipline—something I've personally had to develop over years of business ownership.

Outcomes and New Beginnings

By the end of our sessions, Shortcuts Software had not only a new partner strategy and improved email marketing tactics but also a consistent influx of quality leads from Google. The comprehensive overhaul of their marketing strategies brought newfound consistency and efficiency to their operations.

This venture into the world of B2B marketing culminated in my role as a **Fractional CMO**—a role that merges my coaching expertise with hands-on strategic leadership. This position allows me to engage directly with business stakeholders, providing a unique opportunity to influence and drive business growth collaboratively.

The Birth of Fractional Leadership

The concept of fractional leadership isn't new, but its application in today's business environment is increasingly valuable. As businesses face more complex challenges with tighter budgets, the traditional model of full-time executive hires is giving way to more flexible arrangements.

As a Fractional CMO, I'm able to bring high-level strategic thinking and execution oversight to businesses that couldn't otherwise access this calibre of leadership. More importantly, I can work across multiple businesses, cross-pollinating ideas and approaches that have proven successful in different contexts.

Reflections and Renewed Passion

This journey has been more than just a professional assignment; it was a reawakening of my passion for business. It reaffirmed that the core principles of my career and this book are not only about adapting to change but thriving through it. As markets evolve, so too must our strategies and approaches. The essence of a better business lies not just in its ability to generate profit but to adapt, innovate, and lead in times of uncertainty.

Through this chapter of my career, I have rediscovered the exhilaration of business—a journey of continuous learning, adapting, and most importantly, redefining success. As we look to the future, let us embrace change not as a challenge but as the very fuel that drives our businesses to new heights.

Your Next Evolution

The question now isn't whether your business will face change—it's how you'll respond when it arrives. Will you resist, clinging to what's familiar? Or will you embrace it as an opportunity to evolve?

My experience has taught me that the most successful business owners aren't those who avoid challenges, but those who develop systems and mindsets that allow them to turn challenges into competitive advantages.

Who knows, maybe you might be my next client?

Or perhaps more importantly, perhaps the principles in this book will help you become your own best consultant, equipped with the tools to transform your business regardless of what changes come your way.

Chapter Summary

1. **Change creates opportunity – Market shifts that seem threatening can become doorways to new business models.**

2. **Leverage existing relationships – Your network and past clients offer fertile ground for testing new approaches.**

3. **Structured assessment yields clarity – A systematic approach to analysing your business reveals actionable insights.**

4. **Execution trumps strategy – Even the best plans are worthless without disciplined implementation.**

5. **Fractional leadership provides flexibility – New models of executive support can deliver high-level expertise without full-time costs.**

FREE BONUS:
THE BIG PICTURE CHECKLIST
Fall Back in Love With Your Business

After working with hundreds of established business owners, I've identified the exact pain points that cause entrepreneurs to fall out of love with their businesses.

Your FREE bonus includes:

- The Complete Big Picture Checklist (34-point diagnostic tool)

- Complimentary Ticket to my next Elevate Workshop ($97 value)

- Free Access to the Better Business Community

This toolkit specifically helps established businesses (2+ years) identify:

- Why you're working harder but enjoying it less

- Whether you've built a true business or just bought yourself a job

- The exact area that's causing your biggest frustration

CLAIM YOUR FREE BONUS:

BetterBusinessThatWorks.com/bonus-offer

Use code: **BBTW2025**

RECOMMENDED RESOURCES

Coaching Program

The Better Business That Works coaching program is designed for established business owners who want to grow their business while working less. This program combines one-on-one coaching, group sessions, and practical implementation to help you build systems, delegate effectively, and scale your business.

To learn more or apply for the program, visit
BetterBusinessThatWorks.com

Podcast Series

The Better Business Insights podcast delivers practical advice and actionable strategies from successful entrepreneurs, business coaches, and industry experts. Each episode focuses on a specific aspect of building a better business that works for you, not the other way around.

Listen on Apple Podcasts, Spotify, or at
BetterBusinessThatWorks.com/podcast

ACUA Principle

The ACUA Principle is a framework I've developed to help businesses craft more effective marketing messages. ACUA stands for Availability, Convenience, Utility, and Affordability—the four key areas customers care about before making a purchase decision.

- **Availability**: How quickly can you deliver your product or service?

- **Convenience:** How easy is it for customers to work with you?

- **Utility:** What credibility factors make you the right choice?

- **Affordability:** How can customers fit your offering into their budget?

By incorporating all four elements into your marketing materials, you'll address the most common customer concerns and improve conversion rates. For templates and examples, visit BetterBusinessThatWorks.com/resources

Winning Framework

The Winning Framework provides a systematic approach to tackling any business challenge by asking five key questions in the right sequence:

1. **Why?** - Clarify your objective and motivation

2. **What?** - Define the specific tasks required

3. **Who?** - Identify the best person to handle each task

4. **How?** - Determine the optimal execution method

5. **When?** - Establish realistic timelines and deadlines

This framework prevents you from jumping straight to execution without proper planning, helping you achieve better results with less wasted effort. Download the framework worksheet at BetterBusinessThatWorks.com/resources

Revenue Formula

The Revenue Formula is a practical tool for identifying the fastest path to increased business income. It breaks down your revenue into its core components:

Revenue = (Number of Leads) × (Conversion Rate) × (Average Transaction Value) × (Repeat Purchase Rate)

By understanding which factor has the greatest potential for improvement in your business, you can focus your efforts where they'll have the maximum impact. This targeted approach typically yields a 15-30% revenue increase within 90 days.

Get the Revenue Formula calculator at BetterBusinessThatWorks.com/resources

Wealth Dynamics

Wealth Dynamics is a personality profiling system developed by Roger Hamilton that helps entrepreneurs identify their natural strengths and limitations. Based on Carl Jung's work, it identifies eight distinct profiles: Creator, Star, Supporter, Deal Maker, Trader, Accumulator, Lord, and Mechanic.

Understanding your Wealth Dynamics profile helps you:

- Focus on business activities aligned with your strengths
- Identify what tasks to delegate
- Build a balanced team that compensates for your limitations
- Create flow in your business and life

Take the Wealth Dynamics test at WealthDynamics.com

Systems and Tools

CRM Systems

- **GoHighLevel** - All-in-one marketing and CRM platform perfect for agencies and service businesses

- **Pipedrive** - Ideal for small businesses focused on sales pipeline management

- **HubSpot** - Comprehensive CRM with free tier and excellent marketing automation

- **Zoho CRM** - Cost-effective option with extensive customisation

- **Salesforce** - Enterprise-level solution for complex businesses

Autoresponder and Email Marketing

- **GoHighLevel** - Complete marketing automation solution for agencies and businesses

- **ActiveCampaign** - Powerful automation with reasonable pricing

- **MailChimp** - Great for beginners with a generous free tier

- **ConvertKit** - Designed specifically for creators and digital product businesses

- **GetResponse** - All-in-one marketing platform with landing pages and webinars

Project Management

- **Trello** - Visual, card-based system for managing tasks and projects
- **Asana** - Flexible project management for teams of all sizes
- **ClickUp** - Feature-rich platform combining tasks, docs, and goals
- **Monday.com** - Customisable workflows for various business processes

Other Essential Tools

- **Read.ai** - AI-powered meeting assistant that analyses engagement and provides transcriptions
- **Loom** - Video messaging tool for quick instructions and feedback
- **PandaDoc** - Streamline proposal creation and contract signing
- **Xero/QuickBooks** - Accounting software for financial management

Recommended Books

- Simon Sinek - Start With Why
- Ben Hardy - Who Not How
- Richard Koch - The 80/20 Way
- James Clear - Atomic Habits
- Jack Canfield - Success Principles

- Robert Kiyosaki - Cashflow Quadrant

- Tim Ferriss - 4 Hour Work Week

- David Allen - Getting Things Done

- Dale Beaumont - Secrets Exposed (series)

- Allan Dib - One Page Marketing Plan

- Grant Cardone - Sell or Be Sold

- Brian Tracy - The Psychology of Selling

- Zig Ziglar - The Secrets of Closing the Sale

- Gary Chapman - 5 Love Languages

How to Set Up a Virtual Assistant

Our comprehensive guide walks you through the entire process of hiring, onboarding, and managing a virtual assistant, including:

- Where to find reliable VAs (Philippines, Eastern Europe, or local)

- Interview questions and skills assessment techniques

- Setting up communication systems (VOIP, email, project management)

- Creating standard operating procedures and training materials

- Payment methods and contractual considerations

- Tools for time tracking and performance management

Download the complete guide at BetterBusinessThatWorks.com/resources

How to Improve Your Website Conversion Rate

This practical guide provides step-by-step instructions for optimising your website to convert more visitors into leads and customers. Topics include:

- Conducting effective user testing to identify friction points

- Creating compelling calls-to-action that drive action

- Optimising your lead generation forms for maximum completion

- Implementing trust indicators and social proof

- Creating effective landing pages for different traffic sources

- Setting up proper tracking to measure improvement

Access the conversion optimisation toolkit at BetterBusinessThatWorks. com/resources

For additional resources, templates, and tools to help build your better business, visit BetterBusinessThatWorks.com/resources

ALEXEI KOULESHOV
AUTHOR PROFILE

International Author, Digital Marketing Expert, and Business Growth Coach

Alexei is an international author, digital marketing expert and business growth coach.

He is the founder and managing director of Your Easy Web Solutions, a national company with offices in Brisbane, Melbourne, and the Gold Coast. Alexei and his team have been helping a diverse range of businesses to optimise their digital marketing campaigns and grow their revenue since 2007.

Alexei also owns a number of businesses and partners with other businesses. These businesses include trade, domestic services, and online stores. He leverages his expertise in sales and marketing to drive his businesses and help those he works with.

Being involved in a number of businesses himself allows Alexei to understand the customer journey as well as other aspects of the business that many other consultants don't come across. This involves operations, team motivation, strategic marketing campaigns and business efficiency optimisation.

Alexei has generated millions of dollars for his clients during that time. His client list includes organisations such as 1300SMILES, Shortcuts

Software, Ella Baché, Snap Fitness and Port Containers. He is a sought after speaker and has presented at numerous conferences internationally, and is a member of Business Network International as well as being a prestigious accredited Google Partner.

In addition, Alexei actively contributes to his community. He was a member of the Mud Army cleaning up after the 2022 Brisbane floods, and he supports the Starlight Children's Foundation. He is a board member of his local soccer club and runs a hiking group with the aim of helping men to improve their mental health.

In his spare time, Alexei is a sports fanatic. His favourite sports are fencing, soccer, sailing, Brazilian Jiu-Jitsu and cycling. Through his marketing and consulting skills and passion for travel, he's travelled to various countries such as the USA, the UAE, Japan, New Zealand, France, Greece, Germany, the Netherlands, Italy, Austria, the Czech Republic, Russia, Belarus, China, Korea, Thailand, Bali, Vanuatu, and New Caledonia.

Alexei is the author of *'Better Business That Works'* and *"Our Internet Secrets"*. He lives in Brisbane.

www.ingramcontent.com/pod-product-compliance
Lightning Source LLC
Chambersburg PA
CBHW071855200326
41519CB00016B/4396